MW01393580

"This book is an intimate glimpse into the family life of one of America's most loved men, Oklahoma's own, Will Rogers. Will's homespun humor, political analysis and the easy way in which he connected with everyone from world leaders to ordinary folks is legendary. Will was called the 'unofficial President of the United States,' and that is how our nation saw him: statesmen, ambassador, and true patriot. Congratulations, Coke, on your book, 'I Called Him Uncle Will,' which allows us to learn more about you and the unique Oklahoma family who nurtured a son who changed the world."

—Honorable, Mary Fallin
Governor of the State of Oklahoma

"I am delighted that Coke Meyer is sharing her childhood memories of the great Will Rogers. There can never be too many stories told of Oklahoma's favorite son. It has been nearly 80 years since Will and Wiley Post died in Alaska and the passage of time sometimes allow us to forget just how important Will was to American life. At the height of his journalism career, his columns appeared in more than 500 American newspapers. One in three Americans read at least one of his articles each week.

Coke's story is special because it includes so many family stories. The world knew Will as a trick roper, movie star, humorist, and columnist. But Coke and the rest of the Rogers family knew him as a father, brother, cousin, and uncle. Coke is to be congratulated for allowing us to see inside the family and know better the real Will Rogers.

—Bob Burke
Attorney, Author, and Member of Oklahoma Hall of Fame

"'Miss Coke', the gracious hostess who herself, 'never meets a stranger' invites us (the reader) to join her and her Uncle Will at 'The Soda Shoppe' to sip sweet memories of an earlier time. Thank you, darling 'Coke', for sharing."

—Minisa Crumbo Halsey,
Award Winning Artist and Author

"As warm and interesting a storyteller as 'Uncle Will', we are blessed with our friendship with 'Coke.' We are honored she is sharing her story."

—Jim Halsey, Oklahoma's Legendary Music Impresario

"Coke Lane Meyer knew Will Rogers. She conversed with her great uncle. She listened to his stories. She sat at the lunch counter with him and enjoyed the ice cream he bought for her and her siblings. Few people today have had such first-person pleasure, such privilege of knowing personally and closely the man who became one of the most famous communicators and entertainers in American history, an impactful, down-to-earth voice of common sense, reason, civility, humor. I Called Him 'Uncle Will' offers a rare intimate glimpse into the life of this extraordinary man and, importantly to him and to others, that of the Rogers family."

—Steven Gragert,
Director, Will Rogers Memorial Museums

Oklahoma's favorite son, The Cherokee Kid, and Cherokee citizen are all accurate descriptions of Will Rogers. The world knew him as one of the most skilled trick ropers of all time, with a sharp wit for political commentary and a smile that transcended the screen of a silent film to make the viewer feel like Will was smiling directly at them. Thus, it is no surprise that through the years many writers have endeavored to capture the legend that was Will Rogers but few have been able to provide insight into the man. No other writer has the unique unvarnished perspective that comes with being there when the studio lights, reporters and cameras are all gone and only family remains. Coke Meyer certainly provides this insight in her book "I Called Him 'Uncle Will".

Coke Meyer exemplifies the Cherokee tradition of storytelling in her biography of her beloved uncle, Will Rogers. The world knew Will Rogers the legend, brought to the world by cameras and radio, but Coke Meyer simply knew her "Uncle Will." Coke's book provides an unparalleled glimpse into the life of the Cherokee who loved all human beings. The Cherokee people take great pride in our efforts to maintain our traditions and strong family ties, and we believe that it is family that can most accurately portray and tell the story of another. Coke Meyer does so with humor and poise that would make her Uncle Will proud.

—Bill John Baker
Cherokee Nation Principal Chief

I CALLED HIM
UNCLE WILL

I CALLED HIM
UNCLE WILL

To a Will Rogers Fan

Enjoy
Doris Coke Lane Meyer
2015

A niece remembers life with her famous uncle, **Will Rogers**

DORIS "COKE" LANE MEYER

TATE PUBLISHING
AND ENTERPRISES, LLC

I Called Him Uncle Will
Copyright © 2012 by Doris "Coke" Lane Meyer. All rights reserved.

No part of this publication may be reproduced, stored in a retrieval system or transmitted in any way by any means, electronic, mechanical, photocopy, recording or otherwise without the prior permission of the author except as provided by USA copyright law.

The opinions expressed by the author are not necessarily those of Tate Publishing, LLC.

Published by Tate Publishing & Enterprises, LLC
127 E. Trade Center Terrace | Mustang, Oklahoma 73064 USA
1.888.361.9473 | www.tatepublishing.com

Tate Publishing is committed to excellence in the publishing industry. The company reflects the philosophy established by the founders, based on Psalm 68:11,
"The Lord gave the word and great was the company of those who published it."

Book design copyright © 2012 by Tate Publishing, LLC. All rights reserved.
Cover design by Leah LeFlore
Interior design by Nathan Harmony

Published in the United States of America

ISBN: 978-1-63418-510-3
Biography & Autobiography
12.07.10

To my children and grandchildren, cousins by the dozens, and generations to come. May they always cherish being part of a wonderful family and our heritage. It is my hope that Uncle Will's impact on Oklahoma and the world will never be forgotten.

Table of Contents

Introduction	13
We Interrupt This Broadcast To Bring You Tragic News …	17
Sunset Farm	31
An Unlikely Star Is Born	53
Granny Lane's Death Hit Us Hard, Especially Uncle Will	75
Uncle Will's Generous Heart	87
Leaving Sunset Farm: Our Move to Bartlesville	101
Will Rogers: A "Friend of Aviation"	113
My Life After Uncle Will	125
Fitting Tributes to a Life Well-Lived	143
Going Home Again: Back To Sunset Farm	155
Special Thanks …	169
Photos	171

Introduction

I was born November 12, 1919 at the cusp of the "Roaring Twenties." Sample headlines from newspapers that year were a fascinating mix of topics that would change history on several levels. One such headline read: *Treaty of Versailles Signed, Officially Ending World War I.* Another reported: *8 Chicago White Sox Players Accused of Throwing World Series.* Here's another: *USA Begins Period of Isolationism.* Also, from that year, came these two headlines: *Nazi Party Formed in Germany* and *Prohibition Given Final Ratification.* Though on a much smaller scale, my arrival on a fall day in 1919 certainly was big news, too, in Chelsea, Oklahoma.

Take Highway 66 and travel north out of Claremore, Oklahoma for about twenty miles and you come to Chelsea. The town sits where two highways intersect: Old Route 66 and State Highway 28. When the town was organized, brick streets were laid in the shape of a spoke wheel with downtown Chelsea as the hub. Town historians proudly boast of two significant facts regarding Chelsea: 1) The first oil well in Indian Territory was erected in August of 1889; and, 2) The parents of Oklahoma's favorite son, Will Rogers, are buried in Chelsea Cemetery. Today, Chelsea is a bustling community of about 2,200 people.

It is fall in Oklahoma as I begin this book. Folks in Oklahoma are grateful when fall arrives; they've had enough of the long, stifling hot days of summer. Fall is a glorious respite, even when the ever present wind picks up and the temperature swings from Indian summer to chilly almost over night. As the leaves are changing once again to vibrant reds and gold, I am sensing how my life has changed, too. My family and friends have always been important, but, in this season of life, I feel a greater need to express my love and appreciation for them. Certainly, if I have gained any wisdom, it has come by learning from past mistakes and surviving life's most challenging circumstances through the years. At ninety-two years of age, time is rushing by now like the view from the window of a fast moving train. I am, of course, unable to stop it or even slow it down. But, if I could freeze moments in my past, those spent in the presence of my Uncle Will Rogers, would be some of the best I would ever know.

Why this book; why now? Some details of my early years may have faded through the years, but, for the most part, my memories remain as vivid as the day they occurred. As a gift to my children and theirs, I wanted to record the memories for two specific reasons. First, I wanted to verify the importance of family. The Rogers family kept traditions, communicated with each other, and expressed genuine love and concern in so many ways. Then, secondly, after hundreds of books written about Will Rogers, I felt I could add personal insight into his legacy through the eyes of a young girl who was both captivated and impacted by his larger than life personality.

Will Rogers was called a cow-puncher; the Cherokee Kid; star of stage, screen and radio; adventurer; columnist; unofficial President of the United States; friend of aviation; worldwide celebrity; Oklahoma's favorite son; America's conscience …

I just called him, Uncle Will.

We Interrupt This Broadcast To Bring You Tragic News . . .

> "You must judge a man's greatness by how much he will be missed."
>
> —Will Rogers

Sometime around noon on August 15, 1935, Wiley Post, the famous American aviator, took off from a tidal lagoon off the coast of Alaska near the tiny town of Walakpi. Post was exploring a possible new mail route from the northern most part of the United States to Russia. He and his equally famous passenger, Will Rogers, became concerned about their position after weather conditions deteriorated on the trip from Fairbanks to Point Barrow, Alaska. They had turned into the lagoon to confirm their direction, then again boarded the plane that had recently been rebuilt by Post. The plane seemed sluggish on take off and reached an altitude of only fifty feet when the engine failed. It descended back toward the lagoon in a downward spiral. The aircraft hit the water, dragging the right wing several feet before the wing sheered off completely. The plane crashed on its back in the shallow water of the lagoon. Both men died on impact. It would be the next morning before the news broke across the country.

I Remember the Day We Heard ...

Back in Bartlesville, Oklahoma, the morning of August 16th dawned still and quiet. Our seven room home at 707 Osage was situated near downtown and directly across the street from Garfield School. All five of the Lane children looked forward to school starting in just a few days.

The dog days of summer had arrived and as the family stirred, the house was already stifling, even with windows open to catch the tiniest breeze. My dad, Gunter Lane, a nephew of Will Rogers, sat reading the Tulsa World newspaper, his ritual every morning before heading out to work. Mother sipped coffee, while Bob, my fourteen year old younger brother, and I finished our morning cereal. I would be sixteen years old soon and excited about starting my junior year in high school. Our younger sisters, Jane, 12, and Maude, 10 years old, were still sleeping. Mimi, our older sister, 17, was not at home that day. She was several miles away serving as a camp counselor for Camp McClintock, a Girl Scout camp in Osage County.

The sudden ringing of the phone on that quiet morning startled all of us. Mother, who was closest, answered and then we heard her say, "Just a moment."

She motioned for our father, and then handed the phone off to him. After listening for a moment, his expression turned grim and we heard him thank the man for the call before placing the receiver down.

"Who was that?" Mother asked.

"The paper," he replied. "Something is coming over the AP wire about Will. He said I'd better come right down."

The newspaper office was only three blocks away from our home on the same street.

Before we could ask any questions, Dad sprinted out to the Ford sedan that sat in our front driveway, shouting back, "Belle, turn on the radio! There may be some news coming through already!"

Mother hurried over to the big Atwater Kent radio that stood against the south wall of our living room, switching it on just in time to hear a solemn-voiced announcer advising us to "stay turned for an important news bulletin." Before the announcement came however, the phone rang again. This time it was Dad reporting back to us from the newsroom of the Bartlesville Examiner.

"It's bad news," he told Mother. "Uncle Will and Wiley have crashed in Alaska. They're both dead. Belle, we'll have to leave for California this afternoon."

As Mother was getting the news directly from Dad by phone, the "important news bulletin" was being reported on the radio. As we heard the news, I sat stunned, trying to process the words:

"Yesterday afternoon around 12 o'clock Pacific time, the plane carrying two beloved Americans crashed along the shore near a small Alaskan village. Wiley Post, the accomplished aviator who was the first man to fly solo around the world in record time and his friend, humorist and newspaper columnist known world-wide, Will Rogers, were taking off when Post's small plane crashed on take off. No announcement yet of funeral arrangements for these two men who accomplished so much; both Wiley Post and Will Rogers made monumental contributions to our country. There will be thirty minutes of radio silence in tribute to the memory of aviation pioneer, Wiley Post and his friend, America's greatest ambassador, Will Rogers."

Radio stations would later go off the air across the United States for half an hour as a tribute to Uncle Will and Wiley Post; even movie screens in theatres coast to coast went dark for several minutes in reaction to the shocking news.

Not possible, was my first thought, *they have made a mistake*. The vibrant, funny, kind, thoughtful, brilliant uncle I knew could not be gone. But I was shaken into reality when my mother, experiencing shock and sadness herself, had to quickly make plans for the trip to California, where Will's immediate family lived at the time and where the funeral would be held.

We were interrupted again and again by phone calls from concerned friends just receiving the news. As the news spread, many folks began showing up at our home in a show of support and genuine concern. In that era before air conditioning our windows and doors were often left open in the summer. I recall how it seemed as though those open spaces were almost instantly crowded with people coming in and out all day, friends and neighbors stopping by with condolences, many bringing food, offering to help in any way. One good friend of the family, Daisy Sauser, drove to Camp McClintock to bring Mimi home.

Our favorite baby sitter, Mary Sunday, was contacted to see if she could stay with us while Mother and Dad traveled to California. Although Mimi and I were old enough to care for ourselves and the younger children, (Mimi was going to be a high school senior and, as mentioned, I would be a junior), Mother felt more comfortable asking Mary to watch over all of us while they were away.

Grieving would be postponed because of the many details that needed to be taken care of. However, the news of Uncle Will's passing hung in the air like a dark cloud as we helped mother prepare for the trip. I was given the task of contacting several ladies to cancel Mother's committee meetings for the next couple of weeks. While I manned the telephone and picked up incoming messages, Mother began to make lists of the things that needed to be done while she and Dad would be away. I don't know how she did everything in such a short time, including packing suitcases for both her and Dad, but somehow she managed.

Meanwhile, my father was making necessary arrangements to be away from his office for a while. He also made sure the car was serviced for the long drive to Pueblo, Colorado where his sister, Laska Luckett and her husband, Hap, lived at the time. From Colorado, the four of them would travel on westward to California to be with Uncle Will's wife and their children.

Mother and Dad Left for California that Night

As Mother and Dad departed, I felt a deep sadness and sense of loss. I was young, but very aware that there were some things that would never be the same. We would never get another phone call from Uncle Will saying he was going to be home for a couple of days and wanted to see everyone. We would never rush over to Aunt Sally's for dinner with Uncle Will and the family while we heard about Uncle Will's travels. We would never again laugh at his antics and homespun humor, or sing along with him at the piano. He died in a cold, remote place, far away from his beloved Oklahoma. The grief was palpable; the entire nation shared our pain.

Mother and Dad drove all night, arriving at Aunt Laska's home for breakfast on the morning of August 17th. Before departing for southern California, they phoned us from Colorado to make sure we were all right and to give us a final admonition:

"Everyone will be watching you to see how you take this awful accident, so be on your best behavior."

We would learn details later of how Aunt Betty, and two of Will and Betty's children, Mary and Jim, received the news of Will's death while up in the northeast. Twenty-two year old Mary had enjoyed a measure of early success while pursuing an acting career, and was starring in *Ceiling Zero*, a summer stock play at Lakewood Theater in Maine. There are two stories circulated about who actually broke the news to them personally. Mary's co-star for the play at that time was budding actor, Humphrey Bogart. One report is that he received the first phone call about the crash and went to the cottage where Mary and her mother were staying to tell them the news. Mary was not there, but Bogart supposedly told Betty of Will's death. However, in a book, later penned by Betty herself, she remembers being told about the crash by the theater manager.

Whenever, or however it was received, the news devastated Will's close knit family who made immediate plans to take the next train bound for California. Will, Jr, the couple's oldest son, was already in California, only hours away from boarding an oil tanker for a trip to the Philippines when he heard the news of his father's death. He would remain there to greet family coming in from across the country. Mary, only a few years older than me, would never return to finish the play in Maine, and in fact, seemed to lose all interest in show business after Uncle Will's passing.

A Family Secret–Aunt Betty's Premonition

Betty Rogers, had done her best to discourage her husband from taking the trip to Alaska with Wiley Post. Instead, she had hoped he would join her in Maine to see daughter, Mary, star in the play which opened mid-August. In fact, she enlisted the help of two of my dad's sisters, Estelle (Stella) and Polly to help convince Will to accompany her to Maine. Aunt Estelle and Aunt Polly drove out to visit Betty and Uncle Will during that summer of 1935. Uncle Will showed them a great time. He had hired a chauffeured car to transport them around Hollywood, taking in the sights, eating at nice restaurants, visiting the 20th Century-Fox lot where they could see movies being made. Each morning, Uncle Will would give his two nieces a rundown of what he'd planned for them; one day, he took them to the studio himself, telling other famous stars, "Meet my folks from Claremore, who are visiting me."

One day, while Will was away from the house, Aunt Betty called the girls in and made an unusual request. "Would you please ask your Uncle Will not to go on this trip with Wiley Post?" she said. "We want him to go to Maine with us to see the premiere of Mary's play. Keep after him. Let him know you think he needs to stay and go to Maine with us."

The girls tried to convince Uncle Will to change his plans, but it was no use. Wiley had spent months in preparation and Uncle Will was committed to making the trip with him. The possibility of seeing Alaska from the air fed Will's adventuresome spirit and he was looking forward to the experience.

It was not widely known, but Uncle Will had already experienced some close calls, some fairly serious scrapes and bumps as a result of flying. Of course, the public didn't know, but Aunt Betty had confided in Mother about some of the earlier mishaps. Some of them may have been aboard Wiley Post's famous plane, the *Winnie Mae*, which many thought had structural irregularities at the time.

My two aunts were not the only ones Aunt Betty enlisted in her effort to keep Uncle Will home. Actor, Joel McCrea and Will had become friends on the set of the 1930 film, *Lightnin'*. From that first big movie role opposite Will, McCrea would go on to become a major star. In an article for the Dec.-Jan. 1979-80 issue of *Modern Maturity*, McCrea wrote, "Just before Will Rogers left on his fatal journey in August, 1935, Mrs. Rogers telephoned me, 'I wish you'd try to talk him out of it,' she said." Later he added:

"I did not tell Will that Mrs. Rogers had asked me to try to talk him out of the Alaska trip. Her anxiety was not, like that of others, based on technical difficulties ... Mrs. Rogers concern was rooted not in aerodynamics but in intuition ...."

I agree. It wasn't Wiley's plane or earlier accidents that troubled Aunt Betty. There was a feeling, an uneasiness about the upcoming trip that she could not shake. Her intense efforts to dissuade him were born out of a deep love to protect him from any danger. Her premonitions were strong and, sadly, they were right.

My aunts returned from their trip to California in early August. A few days later, Aunt Betty went to join Mary in Maine while Uncle Will and Wiley Post flew out to Seattle where they would do last minute checks for the historic trip to Alaska and beyond. It would indeed make history.

Lindbergh Helps Bring the Heroes Home

There would be a lot of speculation about the cause of the crash that took the lives of the two American icons. Post had retired the *Winnie Mae*, the plane used in his record-setting around-the-world flight, and had recently purchased parts of two previously damaged planes to customize an aircraft for the Alaska trip. He took a wing from one Lockheed model and joined it with a Lockheed Orion fuselage. He then added floats to make landing on lakes in Alaska and Siberia easier. Some experts believe the floats Post added to the rebuilt craft were much too large, making the already nose-heavy plane even heavier.

The plane simply could not get enough altitude in the bad weather and when the engine was lost, the flight was doomed.

Charles Lindbergh, another great American hero and aviator of that time, had become a close friend to Uncle Will. Upon hearing of the accident, Colonel Lindberg made all the flight arrangements necessary to have the bodies of the two men flown home from Alaska.

Some say the country hadn't experienced such widespread mourning since the death of president, Abraham Lincoln. Our family's mourning was profound because it was deeply personal. We would miss Uncle Will's wit, wisdom, generosity, and love on a level the public couldn't know.

Thousands Pay Respect to Uncle Will

There is an old newsreel produced by the British press and available to view on the internet that shows thousands of people passing by Uncle Will's casket as he "laid in state" on the grounds of the Forest Lawn Cemetery in Los Angeles. A saddled, riderless horse is shown following Uncle Will's casket. Boots in the stirrups are turned backward. The symbolic tradition was usually reserved for military leaders and fallen presidents, but it was fitting for Uncle Will to be honored in this way given the contributions he had made to his country. There are two explanations given for the tradition of the riderless horse with boots reversed. Mainly, it signifies that the rider will ride no more, then, also, it is a picture of the rider turned to look back once more at his family or those he led. I still marvel at the crowds who came in droves to pay respect to the man, a simple cowboy, who made us laugh at ourselves at a time in history when we needed to laugh.

A small, formal funeral was conducted in the chapel at Forest Lawn for no more than one hundred and fifty of Uncle Will and Aunt Betty's closest family and friends. He would be placed in the mausoleum there temporarily, because Aunt Betty hoped to return Oklahoma's favorite son to Oklahoma for burial as soon as possible.

A public memorial service in tribute to Uncle Will was held at the Hollywood Bowl and attended by thousands. Douglas Fairbanks, Jr. organized the program which was broadcast live by radio across the country. It seemed as if the whole country was focused on remembering Uncle Will in special ways.

Memorial Service in Claremore Broadcast to the Nation

A memorial service was also slated to take place inside the large hangar at the Claremore Airport. Uncle Will had been instrumental in raising interest and funds for building the Claremore Airport. I'm sure he never conceived the possibility of using the hangar in this manner. This service would also be broadcast nationally by radio. Since our parents would not be returning from California until August 21st, I accepted the invitation of our family friends, Mr. and Mrs. Mose Gash to accompany them to the service. Their daughter, Marilee, had been my best friend since the seventh grade. Arriving at the airport, we saw cars parked along every road leading into and around the airport. Mr. Gash parked as close as possible, but, it seemed a mile away as we trudged along with the crowd toward the airport hangar. It was so hot and humid that day that Mrs. Gash kept reminding Marilee and me, "Now, you girls keep your hats on." I'm sure she thought we might get sunstroke if we took them off.

The mood was somber as we entered the hangar. One of the first sights was cousin, Herb McSpadden holding the reins of a beautiful horse; another riderless horse, saddled, with boots turned backward in the stirrups. The horse tossed its mane as the people looked on. The riderless horse had great meaning for some of Uncle Will's special friends present that day. These were friends from Oklahoma and around the country, with whom he had worked the rodeo circuit, rode, roped or drove cattle with in earlier days.

The heat was close to unbearable as folks kept crowding into the Claremore Airport hangar for the memorial service in honor of Uncle Will. Folding chairs had been set up to accommodate as many as possible. The Gash family and I found seats midway in the audience as people kept packing in, literally shoulder to shoulder in every row. Outside, many were turned away as every seat was taken.

I remember the floral summer dress I wore. Mother had spent hours smocking the bodice, adding the special stitching that made it one of my favorites. However, on that August day, the pretty dress stuck to my skin as I waved a funeral home fan furiously in front of my face, praying for some relief. The funeral home fans, featuring an ad for the local funeral home, were snatched up quickly at the entrance of the hangar, but did little to alleviate the oppressive heat. The walk from the car to the hangar had been difficult enough, but inside the closed-in building where there was no chance of a breeze, it was brutal. People stirred uncomfortably in the seats as the broadcast began.

Unlike the sophisticated sound systems we have today, the microphones of that period made the speaker sound hollow, distant, and the acoustics in the hangar produced an echo which made listening difficult. I'm sure folks listening by radio heard the ceremony better than we did in the hangar.

Commentator, Glenn Condon, who would later be on hand for the opening of the Will Rogers Memorial, was the local announcer for the program. All other speakers would be speaking by way of radio hookups from various sites across the country. Humorist, Irvin S. Cobb, who'd originally created the Judge Priest character Uncle Will played in the movies, shared his memories of Uncle Will. Stage and screen star, Al Jolson, also eulogized him. Various others offered condolences. Then, when President Franklin D. Roosevelt spoke by radio, people strained to hear his words. They were sincere, heartfelt words which became the voice of a nation grieving for a man who had lifted our spirits so many times. President Roosevelt's words were similar to those he would speak later, again by radio, at the dedication of the Will Rogers Memorial later in 1938:

"This afternoon we pay grateful homage to the memory of a man who helped the nation to smile. And after all, I doubt if there is among us a more useful citizen than the one who holds the secret of banishing gloom, of making tears give way to laughter, of supplanting desolation and despair with hope and courage. For hope and courage always go with a light heart. There was something infectious about his humor. His appeal went straight to the heart of the nation."

The entire service lasted no more than an hour and a half. People filed out quietly, but didn't rush away. Many stopped in groups to talk; some called out to neighbors or waved at friends from across the way. Marilee and I chatted all the way back to the car. As we walked, I couldn't help but notice the cross section of people that had gathered that day. There were men in business suits, bankers and politicians, ladies sporting the latest fashions, black families, native Americans, farmers and housewives, poor folks wearing their Sunday best, and cowboys, many of whom I knew by name.

I was a sixteen year old girl already embracing memories of the man they all had come to honor–memories I knew would last a lifetime.

> "I'm just an old country boy in a big town trying to get along. I have been eating pretty regular, and the reason I have been is because I have stayed an old country boy."
>
> —Will Rogers

Sunset Farm

> "I am mighty happy I'm going home to my own people, who know me as 'Willy, Uncle Clem Rogers' boy who wouldn't go to school but just kept running around the country throwing a rope, till I think he finally got in one of them shows.' They don't know how I make a living. They just know me as Uncle Clem's boy. They are my real friends and when no one else will want to hear my measly old jokes, I want to go home. It won't make no difference to them."
>
> —Will Rogers

So who am I, and how do I fit into the Rogers clan? My given name is Doris Lolita Lane Meyer, but, I have answered to the nickname "Coke" for as long as I can remember. The easiest way to tell folks about my connection to the Rogers family tree is to explain that my grandmother, Maud Rogers Lane, was a sister to Will Rogers. Perhaps, seeing the family tree information on paper makes it easier to identify the different branches. I have included it on page 50–51.

The family is proud of our native-American roots. Will's father, my great-grandfather, Clement Vann Rogers, was a member of the Cherokee nation who contributed much to Oklahoma's history. The son of pioneers from Georgia, he established a vast ranch around the Verdigris River, and, after fighting in the Civil War, returned to his cattle operation in the northeastern part of Indian Territory. Uncle Will and his siblings would be born near a town known as, Oologah, an Indian term meaning, "dark cloud." Clem Rogers served as a Cherokee senator and judge and was named the Cooweescoowee District's representative to the Oklahoma Constitutional Convention in 1906. The next year, Oklahoma Territory and Indian Territory were combined to create, Oklahoma–the 46th state of the Union. The area including great-grandpa's ranch was named Rogers County in his honor.

As the story goes, the boundaries of Rogers County did not originally include the town of Chelsea. Clem Rogers petitioned legislature to include the town because two of his daughters, Sally Rogers McSpadden, and my grandmother, Maud Rogers Lane lived there. The request was granted and Rogers County remains one of the odder-shaped counties in the state because of the inclusion of the town.

Will's mother, Mary America Sherimcher also had native-American roots. You may recall one of Uncle Will's famous lines, "My ancestors didn't come over on the Mayflower, but they were there to meet the boat." We also had ancestors from Wales and England, Scotland and Ireland and Germany. As Grandfather Lane used to say, when asked about his heritage, "We are Americans."

Will Rogers had three older sisters: Sally, Maude, and May. Maude, my grandmother, was the fourth child born to Clem and Mary Rogers. They had eight children together but only the four would live to adulthood.

Mary, their mother was caring for their daughters who had typhoid fever when she herself became infected and died in 1890. Will was eleven years old at the time. Maud, who would become my grandmother, had a difficult time recovering from the fever. Afterward, she stayed in the home to care for her mourning father and helped to raise young Will, who was ten years younger.

Then, in October of 1891, Maud married a young man by the name of Cap Lane. Cap had attended Kemper Military School in Boonville, Missouri, and earned a pharmacology degree. (Will would attend this same school a few years later). Maude and Cap's wedding was held at the Rogers ranch and among their wedding gifts was a team of horses from the bride's father. The couple settled in Chelsea, where Cap would own and operate Lane's Corner Drug Store for many years. They had three daughters, Estelle (Stella), Ethel (Polly), Lasca (Winkie), and one son. The son, James Gunter (J.G.), was my father.

My Parents Met at Stella's Christmas Party

Jennie Belle Mooney, known as Belle, was a young lady attending school in San Antonio, Texas, studying to be a teacher. She came north to visit her family in Chelsea, Oklahoma in 1913, during the Christmas holiday break. Her mother was already living in Chelsea with an older sister who worked at the local bank. There was also an older married brother who lived with his family in Chelsea, too.

Aunt Estelle, or Stella as we called her, another of Dad's sisters, was known for hosting some of the biggest, liveliest parties in the county. She had invited the Mooney family to the Christmas party to be held in her home that year and in fact, directed Dad, to prepare the surrey and pick up Mrs. Mooney and her daughter, Belle, and escort them to the party.

The party was a huge success, made even more enjoyable because Uncle Will made it home for the festive affair. He brought along sheet music to some of the more popular songs he had heard on the vaudeville stage. Someone offered to play the songs on the piano that sat in Estelle's parlor and soon everyone joined in. As he sang, the young Belle, who had a lovely voice, began to join him because she was familiar with the tunes. It was said that Uncle Will, who always knew how to have a good time, enjoyed the party immensely that evening, especially singing with the pretty visitor from San Antonio who would become my mother.

Mother returned to San Antonio following the holidays, but returned to Chelsea the following spring to stay. The girl with laughing eyes and sunny disposition stole my father's heart from the beginning. She and Dad soon became inseparable and married a couple of years later in April, 1917.

Everyone Had a Nickname—How I Got Mine

My older sister, Ethel Marie, whom we called, Mimi, was born in 1918; I was born the next year on November 12, 1919. My earliest memories include the rented home in Chelsea where we lived while Dad worked for a coal company owned by a man by the name of Peabody. The strip-mining work was done mostly in the Catale and Big

Cabin areas of eastern Oklahoma. Of course, mother was busy rearing the five children that came along regularly over the next few years.

Only a couple of blocks away from our home in Chelsea, sat grandfather's store, Lane's Corner Drug Store on Sixth and Pine. The red-brick two-story building was half a block deep and to a young child, seemed huge. There was a soda fountain with an old fashioned counter covering much of the wall to the left, with big mirrors in the back and marble countertops for the customers. Glasses, ice-cream dishes, and spoons of varying lengths were stacked neatly in front of the mirrors, along with a vase-like container that held paper straws, a shiny napkin holder, and glass jars filled with different flavors of liquid syrup. In addition to the stools at the counter, there were three tables, also marble-topped, where people sat to visit and sip their drinks.

Shelves lined the right side of the place, full of medicines, school supplies, general merchandise, stationary, and fancy things for women like powder and cold creams. Granddad's pharmacy was in the back, where he could look out of a window and see everything that was going on in the store.

Many times, my sister Mimi and I would be playing outdoors when we would get thirsty and think of the cherry phosphates served at Granddad's store. Like a beeline we headed that way time after time.

Among the ingredients Granddad kept in his pharmacy was Coca-Cola syrup, which he used in mixing some of his medicines. Of course, when it was blended with carbonated water, it made a wonderful fountain drink. Early on, with a little cherry syrup added, it became my beverage of choice, Cherry phosphates—cherry syrup and soda water—were fine, but I *loved* Coca-Cola.

In fact, I loved it so much that an old bachelor friend of the family, Dave Cone, gave me a new nickname. Dave frequented the drug store often and seemed to be there whenever Mimi and I arrived. He would lift me up onto the high seat at the soda fountain to order my coke. Earlier, he'd started calling me DoDo, because, he said, "Doris is too formal for a three-year-old girl." But after seeing how I took to my new choice of drugstore libations, he said, "I'm just going to call you Coca-Cola, because that's all you ever drink." The nickname caught on with everyone in the drugstore, and soon spread to my family, who shortened it to "Coke"—the name I still answer to today.

I remember Granddad Lane as a distinguished looking man, often seen around town in a starched shirt, suit and tie. He was a member of the Board of Directors for the bank and president of the Chelsea school board. When we visited the drug store, we would see him at work in the back of the store, wearing an apron to fill prescriptions and mix up the medicines town folk needed.

Granddad had a pleasant smile and seemed quiet to some, but, actually he was somewhat of a homespun philosopher. He was well-read and could engage in conversation with anyone. When special speakers, politicians, or lecturers came to town, Granddad Lane enjoyed visiting with them and sharing knowledge of current events and issues. There were various newspapers, National Geographic and

Harper's Bazaar magazines always stacked on his desk at home and at the store.

Besides working at the drug store, Granddad also farmed and helped Granny Lane with their small dairy business. It was a shock to family and friends when sudden word came that Granddad died of a cerebral hemorrhage on July 19, 1924. He was fifty-six years old.

The Move to Sunset Farm

I was very young when our grandfather died. In the fall of that same year, our family moved out to Granny Lane's place, known as Sunset Farm. The years I spent at Sunset Farm (from age five to ten) would provide countless, dear memories of a special place and time. Mother and Dad would help Granny manage the farm over the next few months until her death which came only a year after we lost Granddad Lane.

I don't know exactly how Sunset Farm was named, but I want to believe it had something to do with our spectacular Oklahoma sunsets; incredible hues not found anywhere else except on the open plains of the Midwest. You could sit atop the hill or catch a glimpse of the sun going down from the front porch. It was like a beautiful finale to a perfect summer day—reds, golds mixed up with blue sky and drifting clouds—Oklahoma sunsets are the most beautiful in the world.

Sunset Farm sat on land situated behind the Lane home, a majestic house, especially for that time, only a block from Highway 66 that runs between Chelsea and Claremore. Although it was within the city limits, the farm was a kid's perfect playground with trees surrounding the house, a creek, two ponds, plenty of animals to care for, and fields of crops as far as the eye could see.

Granny Lane's big, old-fashioned three story house made quite an impression. Town folk called it a mansion and it certainly was to me, a little girl moving into the grand house on Maple Street.

Granny Lane's House at Sunset Farm

Downstairs ...

In 1901 a fire destroyed the first home Granny and Granddad Lane had on Sunset Farm. The re-built home with the most up-to-date conveniences, was the regal three-story home we moved into. The house was surrounded by a wrought-iron fence with a gate in front and a walkway to the five steps leading onto a wrap-around front porch. Close to the house was a big cedar tree which Granny decorated brightly each Christmas.

Upon entering the front door, one would notice a long hallway and a stairway leading to the upper floors. A cloak closet and lavatory with a flushing toilet (quite a luxury back then) was located under the stairs. Along the left-hand wall, extending all the way to the bathroom, were wooden pegs for hanging coats and hats.

On the right, off the hallway, was a small parlor which had a sliding door; the kind that disappeared into the wall and could be closed or left open to lead into a small living room area behind. Granny's parlor had a piano and settee. Every elegant home of the time had a parlor area; a special room set aside for private conversations, entertaining a visitor, or for courting. The parlor served another purpose, too. When a family member died, the body was often placed in an open casket and displayed in the parlor of a home prior to the funeral. The term "funeral parlor" came from the fact that families used the parlor as a "viewing" area for visitors dropping by to pay respects to deceased loved ones.

Our move to Sunset Farm took place not long after Granddad Lane had been "layed out" in the parlor shortly after his death. This is one of the reasons my sister, Mimi, would come to hate going into the parlor alone. She took piano lessons and would need to practice on the piano in the parlor, but would always ask me to go sit with her while she practiced. The sight of Granddad Lane's casket placed in the parlor made a profound impression on Mimi. The parlor was always very cold, too, with the radiator set just above freezing. It would be turned up if company was coming and the parlor was going to be open; otherwise, it was pretty frigid in there. Mimi had a harder time convincing me to go in there with her when it was cold, but I'd usually go along and read a book while she practiced.

Like many children before and since, I learned to play "Chopsticks" on the piano. Mimi taught me that one little tune, and that was pretty much it for my repertoire. After trying me out for a couple of lessons, Mrs. Roland, the piano teacher, told Mother—gently, I'm sure—that my talents lay somewhere other than the keyboard. I'm sure Mother was disappointed, but I was relieved. I was kind of a tomboy anyway, far happier playing with my brother, Bobby, or riding our horse, than I was sitting at the piano.

Across from the parlor on the left of the hall was a formal living room. It was a lovely room, with a wood fireplace topped by a gold-framed mirror above the mantle. I would later display the mirror in my own home for many years. The south and west windows of the room had been hung with curtains of filigreed lace glass, along with heavy drapes, and light was provided by electric chandeliers, with crystal bulb holders and strings of lustrous beads connecting them.

I don't recall knowing how Granny Lane acquired all her fine furniture. There was a family by the name of Levine who had a store in Chelsea that sold new and used furniture, so she may have purchased some of it there. It may also have been shipped in–getting goods and furniture from the Sears Roebuck mail-order catalogs was the big thing back then. The pieces also may have been purchased in nearby Tulsa. Tulsa was a growing city at the time with several furniture stores.

From the front formal living room, another sliding door could be open to lead guests into the dining room. Granny's large dining table could accommodate six easily, but, on special occasions and holidays, 10-inch leaves were added so the table could seat as many as sixteen.

Beside Granny's table was a huge sideboard made of rich, dark wood that rose all the way to the ceiling, with beautifully hand-carved forest animals for decoration. There were two shelves on either side, one holding a wine carafe and glasses, and a big mirror back behind the shelves. She kept her tablecloths, napkins, and small teaspoons in the drawers below the top of the sideboard.

She also had a china cabinet near the dining-room table where she stored her crystal glasses, cut glass compotes, and celery/jelly dishes—three things you don't find much in homes any more. This cabinet also held her salt cellars (small dishes that held salt, as opposed to salt *shakers)* and pepper shakers. Sometimes, we kids would appropriate the little spoons from the salt cellars for our tea parties. Above the china cabinet was the plate rail. Running the length of the wall, it held beautiful hand-painted plates and a few souvenir plates as well.

Also in the dining room was a big bay window. Like all bay windows, there was a little alcove made where the panes of glass met. Ours had window seats with cushions, and Granny would always make sure the newest issue of *Collier's Magazine* was there to be perused. Most of the time, though, when we kids visited—before my family moved in to Granny's house—we'd set aside the *Collier's* and the cushions and break out our Crayolas and coloring books or Big Chief tablets. We would come to spend happy hours playing in the alcove by that bay window.

Another sliding door led from the dining room into the kitchen toward the back of the house. Following our move to the farm, the kitchen table was where our family would take most of our meals. That table, large enough for six or eight, had many other uses. It was used for preparing food, visiting over a cup of coffee with neighbors, rolling out pie dough, and my siblings and I would also use it to do our school work. There was a walk-in butler pantry in the kitchen area, called such, even though Granny never had a butler. She just hired occasional help when needed.

Three sets of china as well as glasses were stacked neatly behind the glass doors of the cabinets in the pantry. They shared space with shelves full of canned food that Granny had put up herself. There was always a variety of home-canned fruit and vegetables, including beans, peas, hominy, tomatoes, peaches, and applesauce.

When relatives came, they would swarm around Granny's kitchen table, sitting, talking, laughing, eating delicious meals that included some of Granny's canned goods and homemade bread. Granny kept a couple of highchairs on the back porch for the times when little ones would visit. Usually during holidays, we kids would eat first at the kitchen table, then go out and play while the adults enjoyed a more leisurely dinner in the fancy dining room.

A door from the kitchen exited to a large back porch which extended the entire width of the house. This closed in area, partially screened, served as a work room where the cream separator, dish pans, work tables, pegs for aprons and towels were kept. Usually only visitors or special guests entered the house from the front; family and close friends used the back door entrance. There was also a back stair case used to access the upper floors from the kitchen.

Upstairs ...

The second floor of Granny Lane's home was just as impressive. The first bedroom located on the second floor, was the Rogers Room, so called, because our great-grandfather, Clem Vann Rogers, Granny Lane and Uncle Will's father, came to visit Sunset Farm every weekend.

Grandpa Rogers lived in Claremore, Oklahoma in an apartment located over the bank he helped to establish. He also owned a livery stable there. But when he traveled to Chelsea and Sunset Farm, he always slept in what came to be known as the Rogers Room,

His routine seldom varied. He took the train from Claremore and arrived at the Chelsea train depot each Friday night. He'd stay until Sunday morning, attending church with Granny and Granddad Lane. Then, he'd be taken to Aunt Sallie's home where he'd spend Sunday night before returning to the train station on Monday morning. Great-grandfather made sure whoever had the assignment of carrying him back and forth to the train depot was rewarded with a quarter for their efforts.

In fact, the family patriarch died in the Rogers Room in October of 1911. My father, only fourteen years old at the time, went upstairs to wake him for breakfast and found that he had passed away in his sleep at the age of seventy-two. After great-grandfather Clem passed away, the room was used by Uncle Will and Aunt Betty whenever they came to visit. They had married in 1908 and for the entire time the family owned the house at Sunset Farm, no one but Will and Betty ever slept in that room.

There was also a small bedroom we called the "tower room" because it followed the curve of the north side of the home. Originally the room had belonged to Aunt Estella "Stella." When she moved out, our Aunt Lasca, whom we called "Winkie" took the room. Then, when our family moved to Sunset Farm the tower room became the bedroom Mimi and I shared.

Next was Granny Lane's large bedroom with its own gas fireplace. One special window on the south side of the room consisted of three hundred cut-glass pieces and was intricately beautiful. I recall the way the light coming through the window made of cut glass and lead gave the room a unique, golden glow different from any other room in the house.

Besides the bedrooms on the second floor, there was a small office area between Granny's bedroom and Polly's room. It was used by Granddad Lane to read, write letters or do any paper work needed. There was a roll-top desk, a high-backed rocking chair with a leather seat, and a lawyer's bookcase with glass doors, four shelves high. As mentioned, the Lanes were voracious readers and I recall seeing the spines of all the novels and non-fiction works behind the glass of the old bookcase. An old leather chaise lounge was also placed in the small space and often Granddad Lane slept there.

Once a year, however, Granddad had to vacate this area while it became a "sewing room." Granny hired a woman, probably out of Tulsa, to come and stay at the farm for a month. During that time, she not only made essentials like towels and aprons, curtains, and sheets for bedding, but, she also created all kinds of beautiful dresses, blouses, even under garments and petticoats for all the girls.

Aunt Polly's bedroom was the fanciest by far. Granny Lane made sure her unmarried daughter had a special bedroom whenever she visited. Polly was a teacher who came to stay for weeks at a time, during the summer, on holidays, or in between teaching assignments. Her room was exquisite. Mimi and I loved every feminine detail.

The sleigh bed and dresser were made from cherry wood. A small vanity held treasures like delicate perfume bottles and an ornate hand mirror. A luxurious bedspread and frilly pillows and shams were so inviting Mimi and I would talk about how great it would be to sneak in and jump on that bed, but, we never dared.

Aunt Polly spent much of her teaching career in Bartlesville and Pawhuska, which had been Osage country during the Indian Territory days. Because of that, Uncle Will–who, of course, came from a Cherokee background–would always kid her about marrying a rich Osage Indian. Polly would not marry until 1939 at the age of forty-five. She married a paint contractor from Wichita, Kansas, named Edward E. Hedges. By that time Uncle Will would be gone from us for almost four years, so he didn't live to see for himself that Aunt Polly's new husband, in fact, wasn't an Osage at all—although he *did* have a pretty good amount of money.

A gas-heated bathroom at the end of the long hall on the second floor also had a flushing toilet, a tub with clawed feet, lavatory, chest of drawers, and a small table with bowl and pitcher. I remember mother always cautioning us about the gas heater, and we made sure never to get a towel or clothing near it.

The house was wired for electricity, but, also still had gas lighting. Granny Lane had chandeliers put in when the house was originally built and they used gas. There were also gaslights along the upstairs hall, which were maintained even after electricity came in. Granny Lane's house was one of the few in the area wired for electricity. Aunt Sallie had both gas and electricity and a family by the name of Hogue also had both. I remember the Hogues had a big prefabricated house actually ordered from Sears and Roebuck in 1913. Their house was the first to have electric lights and I believe they had the first radio in Chelsea, too.

The gas lights were left on all the time; the cost was minimal and they made great night lights for finding our way to the sleeping porch or for trips down to the kitchen for a snack. The gas lights had a coarse pottery base and small mantles, or covers over the glass. These mantles were made of very delicate cloth, shaped somewhat like a baby's sock. They would burn down often and have to be replaced.

Besides gas and electricity, we also used coal-oil lamps, common for lighting most homes back then. They were portable; you could carry them into any room and have enough light to read or sew. The wicks had to be trimmed frequently, and the glass globes needed regular washings, or they'd get smoky.

The main feature of the second story home was the big sleeping porch where we would sleep—even visitors. The room extended out over the back porch and usually held three full size beds and a twin sized bed. The area was screened in, but had heavy canvas curtains that could be rolled up or left down depending on the weather. In the summer the curtains were left rolled up and the entire family slept on the sleeping porch to escape the stifling heat.

Third Floor and Basement . . .

Some of my favorite memories of the house at Sunset Farm would take place on the third floor of the grand home. It was one large open room running the full length of the house and was used mainly for parties and storage. Many times, I would climb the stairs to roller skate on the wood floor from one end of the room to the other.

Granny Lane loved to host parties and the attic was the site for many great times. Every Halloween, Aunt Lasca, her youngest daughter, would invite many young people from Chelsea to a party. Granny and her friend,—aptly named Mrs. Strange, would decorate the attic and then dress up as witches for the gathering.

It must have been such fun! There was dancing and bobbing for apples, and Granny and Mrs. Strange would always have a bowl of peeled grapes for the partygoers to pick up.

"Those are the eyeballs of bad children," Granny would cackle, in her best witch's voice.

A couple of the kids over the years may have been half-convinced she was telling the truth. You had to be a certain age before you could come to the Halloween festivities at Granny Lane's, because younger children could become frightened. Kids in town couldn't wait to grow old enough to be able to attend the parties that were the talk of the town for weeks afterward.

When it wasn't being used as a witch's enclave or another festive occasion, the third floor was storage space for papers and magazines like *Collier's*, *Life*, *Harper's Bazaar*, and *National Geographic,* all stacked neatly to one side. But, the best and most important thing in the attic was Uncle Will's vaudeville trunk. I will mention more about the trunk in the next chapter.

Underneath the grand home was a basement used for storing canned goods and bins of coal for the boiler. There were radiators all through the house, which got their heat from the gas heater in the basement. That was also what heated our water. Granny had a hired hand living on the property, along with his family. He was a black gentleman by the name of Monday. One of Monday's duties was to make sure the basement always had a good supply of coal so he could stoke the boiler as needed. Monday would stoke the boiler each morning, afternoon, and night. Monday also served as a preacher for a local black congregation in Chelsea.

Sunset Farm Outbuildings . . .

Sunset Farm had several outbuildings behind the main house. There was a garage, a big red barn, a smoke house, an outhouse, hog pen, chicken house, a small work shed and also a small house where Monday and his family lived. Monday, who was also a preacher, worked faithfully for Granddad and Granny Lane for many years. Monday, his wife and three children (two boys and a girl) all lived in the little house. The home had nice windows, a front and back entrance, and a wood stove with a smoke stack in the center of the house. I also recall a young black girl by the name of Lilly who came in to do laundry and ironing. She would sing and hum while ironing. Even before we moved to Sunset Farm, I remember visiting Granny Lane and listening to Lily sing as I played nearby.

The big barn had stalls for milking cows and a big pulley used for bringing bales of hay up for storage. As we made Sunset Farm our new home, my sisters, brother, and cousins quickly learned how we could have hours of fun by swinging out on that pulley or by using the stacked bales of hay to play "King of the Mountain." We chased each other through tall grass, played hide-and-seek in the corn field, and rode horses across the expanse of Sunset Farm. The farm would provide the setting for hundreds of adventures and experiences we would treasure for a lifetime.

Dad still had his job at the strip mines when we moved to Sunset Farm. Once, he broke both of his ankles in an accident while mining, and from then on maintained that cowboy boots were the only comfortable shoes he could wear. Of course, he would help Granny out as much as possible when he was home, but most of the daily chores fell to Monday, Mother and us kids.

Uncle Will and his wife, Aunt Betty, would come and visit at Sunset Farm whenever he could get away—but by this time he was gaining in popularity as a performer, movie star and columnist. He and Betty traveled extensively, also. Everyone in the family looked forward to their visits. Uncle Will had already purchased property in the area and referred to it often as the place he would build his retirement home. The call to return to Oklahoma and life among those who loved and knew him best remained strong throughout the years. None of us could speculate that he would never have the opportunity to live out his last years in his beloved home state.

We embraced our new home at Sunset Farm, but in a few months, we began to realize that Granny Lane was not well. All of us had assigned chores as we helped with the house, the crops, the canning, but, more and more, our time was spent in caring for Granny Lane who was growing weaker everyday.

CAP & MAUD LANE FAMILY CHART

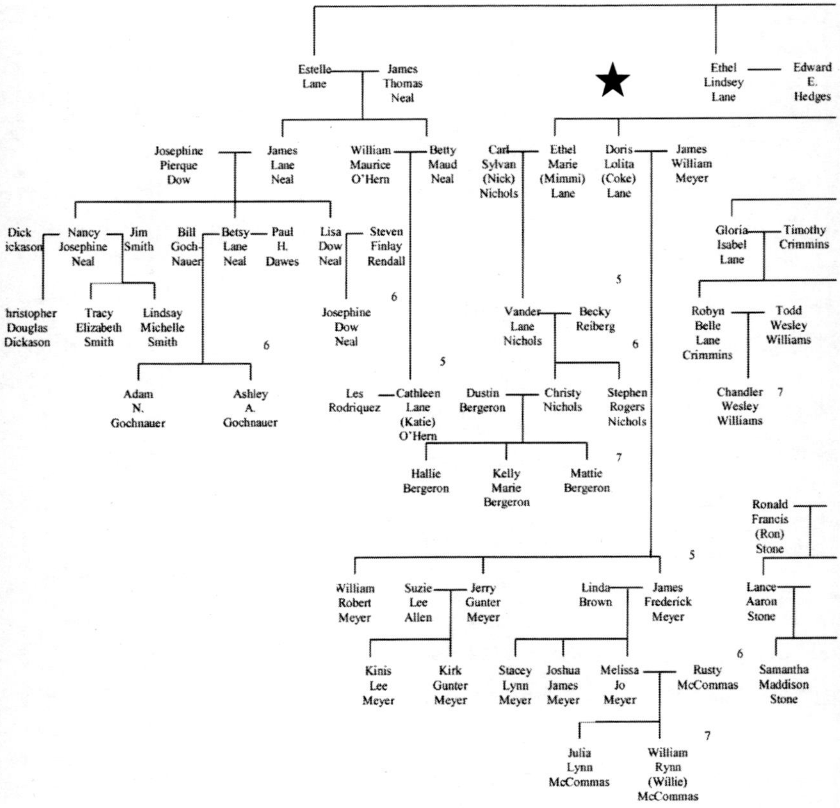

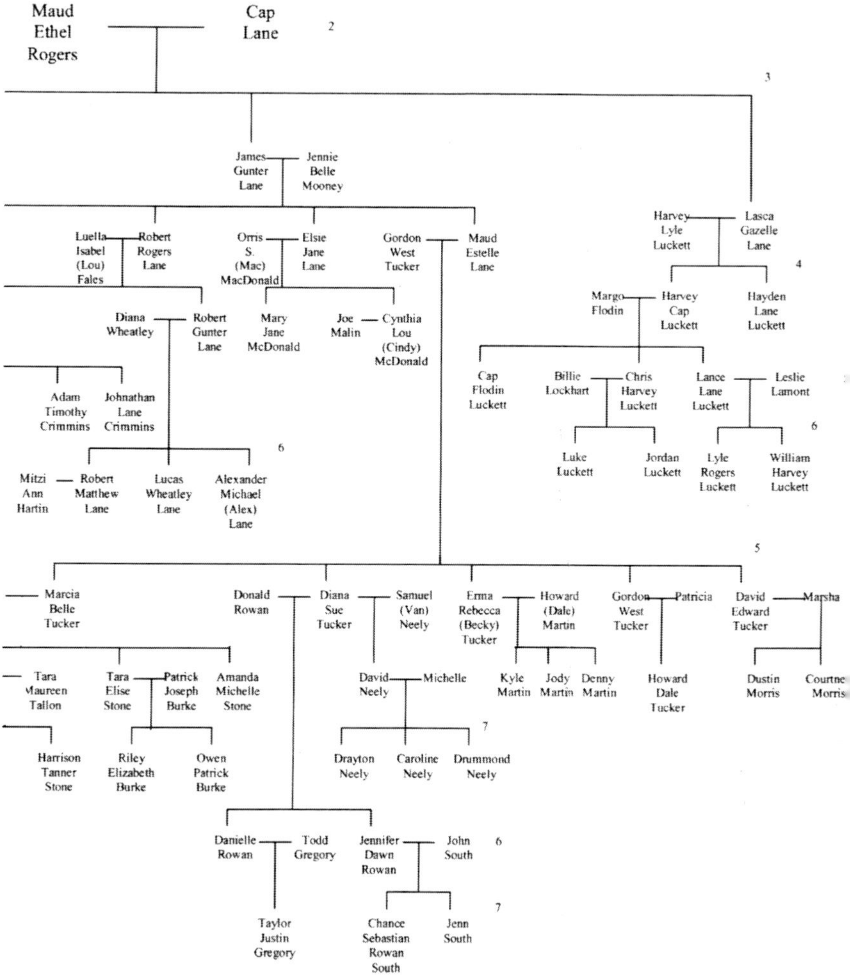
Maud Ethel Rogers
Cap Lane
2
3
James Gunter Lane
Jennie Belle Mooney
Harvey Lyle Luckett
Lasca Gazelle Lane
Luella Isabel (Lou) Fales
Robert Rogers Lane
Orris S. (Mac) MacDonald
Elsie Jane Lane
Gordon West Tucker
Maud Estelle Lane
4
Margo Flodin
Harvey Cap Luckett
Hayden Lane Luckett
Diana Wheatley
Robert Gunter Lane
Mary Jane McDonald
Joe Malin
Cynthia Lou (Cindy) McDonald
Cap Flodin Luckett
Billie Lockhart
Chris Harvey Luckett
Lance Lane Luckett
Leslie Lamont
Adam Timothy Crimmins
Johnathan Lane Crimmins
6
Luke Luckett
Jordan Luckett
Lyle Rogers Luckett
William Harvey Luckett
6
Mitzi Ann Hartin
Robert Matthew Lane
Lucas Wheatley Lane
Alexander Michael (Alex) Lane
5
Marcia Belle Tucker
Donald Rowan
Diana Sue Tucker
Samuel (Van) Neely
Erma Rebecca (Becky) Tucker
Howard (Dale) Martin
Gordon West Tucker
Patricia
David Edward Tucker
Marsha
Tara Maureen Tallon
Tara Elise Stone
Patrick Joseph Burke
Amanda Michelle Stone
David Neely
Michelle
Kyle Martin
Jody Martin
Denny Martin
Howard Dale Tucker
Dustin Morris
Courtne Morris
7
Harrison Tanner Stone
Riley Elizabeth Burke
Owen Patrick Burke
Drayton Neely
Caroline Neely
Drummond Neely
Danielle Rowan
Todd Gregory
Jennifer Dawn Rowan
John South
6
7
Taylor Justin Gregory
Chance Sebastian Rowan South
Jenn South

An Unlikely Star Is Born

> "Every time they make a joke it becomes a law; and every time they make a law it becomes a joke."
>
> —Will Rogers

By the time we moved to Sunset Farm in 1924, Uncle Will had become a household name. It was not an easy road that led him to become a popular humorist, columnist, and radio and movie star.

Will's future certainly would not be determined by his experience with formal education. Much to his father's chagrin, he was not an exemplary student at Kemper Military Academy. Young men who attended Kemper were disciplined for behavior or poor effort in the classroom by "drilling" for hours. Will had amassed so many demerits at Kemper he realized he'd be "drilling for a year straight," should he stay in school. So, he slyly wrote his sisters and asked each for $10 without specifying why he needed the money. After getting the funds to tie him over for a while, he ran away from school and ended up in Amarillo, Texas where he tried to get work on various ranches. Finally, Will was hired as a cowboy on a ranch owned by Ewing Hassell. He would be paid $30 a month and given room and board on the ranch. When Hassell determined who the young man was, he wrote Clem Rogers, Will's father, to tell him his son was safe and asked, "What shall I do with him?"

The patriarch of the family wrote back, "Put him to work and see that he earns his money."

He must have earned his keep. Will worked hard on the ranch and participated in a large cattle drive for Hassell, before he and a friend left for Argentina in 1902. When he left the ranch, Will took along a letter of recommendation Hassell had written for him.

Seeking adventure and faraway places, the young men spent a half year trying to make it as "gauchos" and ranch owners, but the pay was so low, they soon had diminished funds and had to go separate ways. Will sent his friend home with tablecloths, scarves, and handkerchiefs for his sisters and the girls in the family. He later recounted how he had spent that first night after splitting with his friend, alone in a park with absolutely no money for hotel or food. The next day, he went down to the wharf and offered to baby sit horses on a boat headed to South Africa. After arriving there, he joined up with Texas Jack's Wild West Show where he was billed as "The Cherokee Kid," and performed his roping tricks. Wild West shows, very popular for the first decades of the 20th century, were part-circus, part-rodeo affairs, often with a cast of hundreds, bringing patrons all over the world a taste of the American West. Uncle Will traveled to New Zealand and Australia with the show, and then saved up enough money to return home through San Francisco and finally back to Claremore after having gone around the world, all before he was twenty years old.

Although his education was limited, Uncle Will had an insatiable curiosity. His personal experiences, observations and love for travel were his gateways to learning, plus he would read everything he could lay his hands on. Before the days of airplanes and automobiles he had to travel either by horse, train, or steamboat. The experiences of his youth laid the groundwork for his lifelong desire to see new places and understand other people and cultures of the world.

Will Rogers, also, had an intense drive to perfect his skills. He would practice for hours on end, working on the rope tricks that would one day make him famous. In 1905, back in the states, Will joined Colonel Zach Mulhall's Wild West Show as a fancy roper and in October of that year played his first vaudeville bill in Chicago.

Ask anyone under 70 years of age what vaudeville was and the response likely as not will be a blank stare. Some on the older end might remember something about how many stars of early television came from the vaudeville stage, or know that it was some sort of live entertainment. In the early part of the 20th century, vaudeville flourished throughout the country, with hundreds of performing troupes crisscrossing America. The various dancers, actors, comedians, singers, jugglers played to audiences in palatial theaters and ramshackle small town venues. For months at a time they were on the road, catching outbound trains after each performance to travel to the next engagement.

One incident during a Mulhall show in April, 1905 at Madison Square Garden in New York City gave Will a boost in popularity. An 800-pound horned steer broke from the arena floor, jumped a gate and bolted into the stands sending spectators shrieking and running for cover. Several of Mulhall's cowboys took out after it, but, it was Uncle Will who roped the creature and led it back to the ring. The incident was reported in the newspapers the next day and brought Will more attention from the vaudeville producers.

After eight years of courtship, mostly done by correspondence, Uncle Will and Aunt Betty married in November of 1908 in Rogers, Ark. She then accompanied him on the vaudeville circuit. At some point, the rope and horse in Will's act began to give way to more humor and comments on current events and politics. He would appear on stage dressed in cowboy attire, then start twirling his lasso. His blue eyes would twinkle as he turned to the audience with opening comments, "Well, what shall I talk about tonight? I ain't got anything funny to say. All I know is what I read in the papers." He then made quips and jokes about what was going on in the world and around the country. The audiences enjoyed his Oklahoma drawl and homespun insights. In 1912, Will appeared in his first Broadway show.

In 1915, he was booked for a cabaret show on the roof of the New Amsterdam Theater and started a long and prosperous relationship with the legendary vaudeville producer, Florenz Ziegfeld. Will's witty commentary kept America laughing during the dark days of World War I from 1914 to 1918.

It was in 1916 that Uncle Will spoke at a Friars Club meeting in Baltimore which was attended by Woodrow

Wilson. The attendees, including the president, rolled with laughter at his topical humor and he received rave reviews. By 1919 he was appearing regularly in the Ziegfeld Follies along side fellow great performers like Fanny Brice, W. C. Fields, Marion Davies, Ann Pennington and Al Jolsen. It was the same year, 1919, when he left the Follies to appear in a silent film produced by Samuel Goldwyn. His first books were also released that year, *The Cowboy Philosopher on the Peace Conference* and *The Cowboy Philosopher on Prohibition.*

Two years before we made the move to Granny Lane's Sunset Farm, Uncle Will began to write daily and weekly newspaper articles. Written in the manner in which he spoke, the spelling and grammar were not perfect, but, newspapers across the country carried his articles and Will gained many new fans. The errors in his writing were left uncorrected per Will's request: "Just run 'er the way she lands."

By 1925 Uncle Will had appeared in another silent film for legendary film director, Hal Roach and also began a nationwide lecture tour. Then, in 1930, his popular radio broadcasts were heard and enjoyed by millions. He would make more than 40 silent films, then, between 1929 and his death in 1935, he would star in twenty-one full feature films for Fox Film Corporation. Because of proximity to the movie business he purchased a home with several acres for his family in Santa Monica, but still managed to make it home to Sunset Farm whenever possible. Uncle Will and Aunt Betty had four children: Will Rogers, Jr., Mary, Jim, and Fred. Sadly, Fred died from diphtheria at two years of age. Though we didn't see them often, we stayed in touch with the cousins over many years.

As Will Rogers continued to have a larger and more important impact on the hearts and minds of America, his relatives who lived at Sunset Farm enjoyed his achievements from afar. We were keenly aware and proud of Uncle Will's success, but our family was taught that we did not deserve nor should we expect any special recognition ourselves because of his fame. In fact, we were careful not to treat Uncle Will like a celebrity when he and Aunt Betty visited. Our parents cautioned us not to cling too close to Uncle Will whenever we accompanied him out in public. We were also told never to brag about being his relatives. Later on, talking with my cousins, Clem and Bob Mc Spadden, I would find out they had been warned about the same things. Uncle Will was one of the most famous men in the world in the early 30's and I guess the folks wanted to make sure that none of us got big-headed or self-important about their celebrity relative.

Even though we didn't flaunt it, we knew Will Rogers was not only a renowned newspaper columnist and movie and radio star, but also a favorite uncle who loved us and wanted us to be happy.

Life at Sunset Farm Goes on as Usual

Like most children raised in a rural area, we were busy with school and chores on the farm while Uncle Will traveled the world as an unofficial United States "ambassador." We worked hard, but no one worked harder than Granny Lane. She was up before dawn at 4:30 a.m. to help Monday milk the cows. She used to say that she "wore her clothes out from the inside out" because she had to change them so often. Granny would put on her "milkin' clothes" for milking the cows in the morning, then come in and change clothes to fix breakfast. If she had meetings to go to (she was involved in several volunteer organizations), she would change clothes to attend those meetings. Then she would return home, change to her milkin' clothes for the final milking of the day, then, change again for preparing supper. She'd change to dressier "Sunday church" clothes if we had company for dinner or if she was going out for dinner.

The autumn we moved to Sunset Farm, Mimi started the first grade. I was a year younger, but I wanted to go to school, too, so my folks managed to talk the school administrators into letting me start kindergarten although I wasn't quite old enough. Every week day morning Monday dropped us off at school on his way to deliver milk around town. We would climb aboard the milk wagon along with Monday's three children. Mimi was embarrassed to be seen getting out of the milk wagon so Monday would let her off a block or so from the school. She would meet up with her friend Eleanor Parks and walk the rest of the way. Not me. I'd stay on the wagon until we drew up right in front of the building, then jump out the back, yell 'goodbye' to Monday's kids and join my classmates on the McIntosh school grounds. Monday then would deposit his children at the all-black school in Chelsea. These were the days of strict segregation.

I remember well the morning routine on most school days. We would stand in lines around the flagpole, in order of our different classes. The children recited the Pledge of Allegiance, a teacher would give a prayer, then a recording of a John Philip Sousa march would ring out and we'd march into the schoolhouse like little soldiers.

My sister and I had several responsibilities around the place, before and after school everyday, then, there were some seasonal chores that had to be done. One of those was canning time. I still recall the over powering heat when the weather was hot and made hotter by the boiling water in the kitchen during canning. The jars we used had to be boiled to make sure they were sterile, turning the kitchen into a steam bath. Mother would fill sterile mason jars with foods like string green beans, seal the top tightly then place the jars in the big water cooker full of boiling water. Open kettles on the top of the stove were used for boiling the fruit for delicious jams and jellies. All of us, Granny Lane, Mother, the hired help, even Aunt Polly when she was home, pitched in to get the canning done.

The fruits and vegetables from the latest harvest would be stored for a short period in the cool basement, awaiting the time for canning. I remember how the process with hominy would take a little extra effort. You had to take the corn and soak it in lye water, which was made by running water over fireplace ashes and collecting it. We'd leave the corn in the water until the skin came off, then place the corn on screens removed from the windows and arranged on sawhorses, spreading the soft corn around so it would dry easier. We'd have to put cheesecloth over it to keep the bugs and birds from eating it before we could.

Mimi and I also helped with bottling milk and making butter for the family and also to sell to customers in town. We grabbed aprons hanging off pegs on the wall of the back porch to begin. To this day I can see us washing our hands with a rough bar of lye soap, then, climbing up on a pair of stools to reach the cream separator. Everyday we would have to first clean the grease off the metal discs inside the separator by dunking them in a pair of dishpans, using lots of boiled water. It was not a quick or easy task; it took real "elbow grease."

The cream separator was a bowl rigged up with two spouts and a crank. It would hold about five gallons of the warm milk, which came in directly from the cows. Mimi and I would take turns turning the crank, and the milk would flow over a special float, separating the cream from the milk. One of the main reasons for milking cows was to have the milk fat, or cream, which contained most of the energy of the milk, and of course, was used to make butter.

This was hard work for young girls, but we managed. You had to turn the crank at just the right speed; that was the whole secret. When operating correctly, cream would come out of one of the spouts, and what we called "separator milk" out of the other. Often, we gave the separator milk to the farm animals to drink.

Granny had churns for making butter from the cream, along with a wooden press, which would form the butter into uniform bricks. In addition to making sure the separator blades were spotlessly clean, (they would spoil the milk if they weren't), Mimi and I did our share of churning and scraping the butter off the paddles and into the press.

As mentioned, Granny Lane's small dairy operation would sell the butter we made and, of course, the whole milk too. We'd help to bottle the milk, without separating the cream, and the cream would rise to the top of each bottle. (That's where the old saying, "cream rises to the top' comes from.) Homemakers and other customers, then would spoon the cream out of the bottle and churn it themselves to make their own butter. Sometimes they'd whip it up for a desert topping. The milk was for cooking and drinking.

There were so many other chores at Sunset Farm that had to be done. In addition to other responsibilities, my sister and I fed the chickens and gathered the eggs everyday, and were responsible for feeding the dogs and cats on the farm. We never expected to be paid for our hours of labor; it was just life on the farm. I'd be fifteen years old and gone several years from Sunset Farm before I'd see my first allowance.

The Folks Get to See Uncle Will in Action

Around 1925 when Uncle Will started his nationwide lecture tours he was going into towns and cities all across America making appearances sponsored by women's clubs, society groups, and other organizations. Will was all for the idea. He said, "I want to get out and talk to America. I want to see how America is living." He was accompanied by a male quartet who were recording artists at the time. The organizers of the tour had put them on the bill because conventional wisdom dictated that you needed music included in any touring show. The quartet would sing, then Uncle Will would come out on a bare stage and talk for an hour or so, often beginning by pointing out to the audience that "a humorist entertains and a lecturer annoys."

The first stop in Oklahoma for Will's lecture tour was held in Bartlesville, where people gladly paid either a dollar or three dollars to see their native son who'd made good. Among the sold-out crowds were four of Will's nieces and nephews, and their spouses. Before the tour reached Oklahoma, Aunt Betty had called Aunt Sallie McSpadden (Will and Granny Lane's sister) in Chelsea and asked her to invite the family to join the tour for a few days. Dad and mother were among the lucky eight who would join Uncle Will and Aunt Betty for tour stops in Bartlesville, Muskogee, Tulsa, Ponca City, and Wichita, Kansas. They spoke often of how they enjoyed visiting with their cousins and Will and Betty all along the way.

Will's friends, oilmen Frank and L.E. Phillips had a reception for him following the Bartlesville appearance. Later, his friends and relatives from The Pocahontas Club also threw a party for him in Claremore, where he remarked, "When I fail to make them laugh any more, I won't be seen in the places I now haunt. It will be back home here with you people that I will be, to live and die among you."

The Pocahontas Club still exists today with over one hundred and fifty members. It began as a social girl's club in 1899, formed by sixteen young ladies from Cherokee families who attended prestigious boarding schools. After the name for the club was chosen, the girls decided the signature color for the group would be the color red. They also agreed the red carnation would be the club's official flower. Meetings were held every Thursday afternoon during the summer months. Existing purely as a "social" club, young men soon wanted to be included in the events, so the girls allowed "honorary" members of The Pocahontas Club. Thirteen young men were first taken into the club as honorary members and Uncle Will happened to be one of them. He would often say, "I'm an honorary member, and also an 'ornery' member." Uncle Will and Aunt Betty would always feel a special affinity for the group which included life long friends. The club would get a party together anytime they heard that Uncle Will was going to be coming into town.

Uncle Will was receiving accolades for his lecture tour as he traveled from town after town. In Tulsa, the audience response was especially memorable, with an overflow audience of hundreds seated behind Uncle Will on the stage. In a column filed just after the event, he wrote, "Here it was the biggest audience I had ever faced, here it was the *best* audience I had ever faced ... Gee, I was lucky, I fooled them at home."

The audience just would not let him quit that night. According to a letter my mother later wrote about the show, Will talked for two hours and fifteen minutes and people still wanted more. The audience would not leave until he kindly told the folks they *had* to go home because he was "worn out."

Uncle Will's Trunk

I don't recall when Mimi and I first became aware of Uncle Will's big travel trunk we discovered in the third story attic. Inside were big, rolled-up posters, souvenirs from his days on the vaudeville circuits, when he was doing his cowboy/roping act. Underneath those were the special hoof covers, or shoes, worn by Teddy, Will's horse, when they came out on stage together. They were specially made to prevent Teddy from falling on the slick wooden stage, with laces to tie them securely around Teddy's ankles.

The trunk also contained a pair of brown leather chaps and couple of cowboy shirts Uncle Will had worn in his shows. At the bottom of the trunk were a couple of coiled lariats, but, we couldn't twirl them because they were too long and heavy. So, after a little bit of experimenting, we left them in the trunk.

When we wanted to pretend we were vaudeville stars, we would carefully pull out the posters and place them all around the attic. We knew these had to be from Will's earlier days in the business, because he didn't have top billing. His name would appear further down, perhaps fourth or fifth in order and smaller in print then the headliners for that period.

Usually, we would try to recreate the act Uncle Will and Teddy had done—at least as we imagined it was. Bob was our younger brother so he would be pressed into service as Teddy, getting him into a pair of Teddy's special shoes and he'd clop around like a pony. Mimi and I would put on hats and bandanas and try to lasso him with ropes.

When we had cousins over, all of us would wind up in the attic going through Uncle Will's trunk. I remember our Neal cousins, Jimmy and Betty Maud, playing with us there in the attic and our Mooney cousins, too, Maxine, L.E. and Patty—they were old enough to read all the names of the performers and cities listed on the posters.

We may have been a little raucous in our play, but we knew better than to treat anything from Uncle Will's trunk disrespectfully or casually. When we finished imagining ourselves on some stage in a faraway place, we carefully put everything back in the trunk just as we found it. We didn't treat it like we owned it, we knew it wasn't ours. It wasn't even Granny Lane's–it was Uncle Will's.

I would later visit with Jimmy, Uncle Will's youngest son, and he would tell me about another trunk he discovered at their ranch in California. This trunk, however, held an unusual item: a unicycle. It turns out that for a while Will used a unicycle for his act. He would hop on, then do some rope trick while perched atop. The story related to us was that there was also a Chinese act in the vaudeville troupe at that time who used a unicycle, too. They also had a portion of their act which included a roping demonstration. Will went to them after a show and made a deal, "You stop using the rope trick and I'll stop using the unicycle." So, the unicycle was discarded and had been stored in this trunk in pieces. Jimmy, Will's son, who was a young teenager at this time, and a friend worked to put the unicycle together again and were just about ready to "test it out," when Uncle Will saw them tinkering with it.

"What are you boy's doing?" he asked.

"Well, Dad, we are going to try and ride this thing."

Before they knew it, Uncle Will spun it around, jumped on and rode it like he was born to ride the unicycle. It astonished the boys since it had been years since Will had used it in his act.

The trunk at Sunset Farm, and its' contents, would eventually be shipped to Will's family after we sold the farm. To this day, I recall the fun we had in the attic pretending to be as famous as Uncle Will. Later, some of the items in the trunk, like Teddy's special shoes, ropes, the posters, would be displayed at the Will Rogers Museum in Claremore.

The smokehouse on Sunset Farm also became a place to pretend we were stars of screen and stage. During summer months the smokehouse was cleaned out to be ready for storing the ham and variety of meat for the family. Inside the smokehouse was a large table that, when empty, made a great "stage" for our productions. Mother gave us some old hats, shoes, and dresses to serve as costumes for our acts. We would practice songs or dances on our makeshift stage, then invite family and friends in and charge them a few pennies or a nickel to see the show.

Dad Was Once Almost in Show Business, Too

Dad came very close to being in show business himself for a short time. Uncle Will appeared in a silent film series which featured his European travels. These one-reel humorous documentaries, a dozen of them, not only starred Will, but he wrote the title cards as well. Released in 1927 by the Pathe` company, the film titles were similar to these: *Hiking through Holland with Will Rogers* and *Hunting for Germans in Berlin with Will Rogers.*

While in production, the producer, Carl Stearns Clancy, mentioned that he would like to find a "stand-in" for Uncle Will. Stand-ins were common then and now. These individuals take the starring actor's place while camera crews and technicians do tedious work like setting up scenes or working on lighting and also acted as stunt men. The availability of a stand-in relieves the actor in these situations and the process is less tiresome. Aunt Betty mentioned to Clancy that she knew just the right person, a relative who resembled Will,

"It's Will's nephew, Gunter Lane," she said. "He lives back in Oklahoma and he'd be perfect."

So, Clancy sent a telegram to dad, followed by a phone call explaining Aunt Betty's suggestion, and soon a contract arrived in the mail. There was only one problem: No one had told Uncle Will of the arrangement.

When Aunt Betty told Will about possibly using Dad for a stand-in, he nixed the idea quickly.

"No, there's no way I won't do my own work."

Uncle Will did not want a stand-in even for long shots. His attitude I'm sure had something to do with his strong work ethic, and concern about cheating the public in any way. It may also have sprung out of sincere concern for us. He told my father later, "Gunter, Hollywood isn't a place for you to raise your fine family."

Whatever the reason, Dad was disappointed at missing a shot to be involved in show business by the slimmest of margins. Will made up for not using my father in the films; he invited him to take a trip of a lifetime. He called the house with the information,

"Gunter, American Legionnaires all over the U.S.A. are getting on a ship to go to Paris to celebrate the tenth anniversary of the Armistice. If you can get off work, I'll send you over with 'em."

Uncle Will knew Dad was a World War I veteran and a past commander of Chelsea's American Legion post which made him a perfect candidate to take the trip. That year, 1927, all of the arrangements were made and Dad boarded a train to New York for a stay at the famous Waldorf Astoria Hotel before departing with many fellow veterans and their families. Uncle Will paid all expenses for the wonderful trip Dad would talk about for many years. I am convinced the trip was Uncle Will's way of making up for not using Dad as a stand-in.

A few years later, Dad did have an opportunity to *stand-in* for Will in a manner of speaking. In the early '30's Dad and mother were attending the state American Legion convention in Muskogee when convention organizers approached him during the evening banquet,

"Gunter, our speaker has fallen through for tonight's program following the banquet. Would you save us by taking the stage and impersonating Will Rogers? We'll just pretend that was what was planned all along," one of the men said.

"I've never done anything like that. I couldn't do it."

The men were adamant, "You look like him and you know what he does. You can do it. If you don't, our names are mud, because we won't have a program at all."

Recalling it later, Dad said he sure didn't want to get up on that stage and try to talk like Will Rogers, but he hated to let those fellows down, so he agreed. He went on stage in Muskogee as his famous uncle and while it was clearly announced beforehand that a substitute for Will Rogers was going to speak, he did such a good job some attendees actually believed it really was Will Rogers. Needless to say, the committeemen were thrilled at the outcome.

Christmas at Sunset Farm

As Uncle Will's fame continued to grow and extend even beyond the United States, we were making precious memories ourselves. Some of the ones I hold most dear are the Christmases spent at Sunset Farm even before we called it home. In addition to Granddad and Granny Lane, there was Dad and Mom and us kids, Granny's two married daughters, Aunt Stella Neal and Aunt Winkie Luckett, and their families would make it out to the farm. Aunt Polly wasn't married at the time and she would be in for the holidays. Uncle Will did not travel to Sunset Farm for Christmas after moving to California. He spent the holidays there with his family, but his Oklahoma family would hear from him during Christmas and he and Aunt Betty would send gifts our way.

Uncle Will was known for waiting to do his shopping until Christmas Eve. He'd go out in the afternoon, select his gifts and take them home and wrap them in time to put them under the tree for Christmas morning. I can't remember all the gifts that Uncle Will and Aunt Betty sent us each Christmas during our Sunset Farm years, but

I do recall how boxes would arrive from their California address through out the year, usually full of clothes. Sometimes, everything was fresh from the clothing store. Other times, it would be good-as-new hand-me-downs from our cousin, Mary. Once, after Will and Betty had taken a trip to Scotland, a box arrived in Chelsea with some beautiful Scottish sweaters and skirts they had picked out for us.

Mimi and I were always excited when one of these big parcels came in the mail. I don't think Uncle Will had much to do with actually putting the contents together, though. They were mostly assembled by Aunt Betty and her sister, Theda, whom we called Aunt Dick (and I have no recollection how she received the nickname). Aunt Dick, who never married, stayed with the Rogers family in California and took care of the children when needed while they were growing up. Her presence in the Rogers household become increasingly valuable as the demands of Uncle Will's career grew. Whoever prepared the packages, Mimi and I were elated when they arrived.

The Christmas tree at Sunset Farm was placed in Granny Lane's parlor each year on Christmas Eve. We never got to see our tree until after supper on Christmas Eve. Dad would go into the parlor, shut the door, and get the tree decorated. He'd call us when finished and we'd run in to see the tree for the first time, then all the cousins would sit down excitedly beside the tree and the colorfully wrapped presents underneath. A designated person would hand out all the gifts. With all the family in attendance the gift-opening took a good long time.

After presents were opened we climbed into our double beds, which had feather comforters and, in the winter, hot bricks under the covers to keep us warm. We'd fall asleep dreaming about what Old Saint Nick was going to leave us on Christmas morning. Of all the gifts Santa dropped off at Sunset Farm on Christmas day, my favorite was the brand new pair of roller skates mentioned earlier. I would spend hours skating across the floor of the third story attic. It was like having my own personal skating rink.

Just as memorable as any gift, though, were the meals Granny would fix for the family on Christmas day. After we kids had roused the household at an impossibly early hour, checking out what Santa had left, there was breakfast—which included a delicacy you don't see on too many holiday menus any more: fried pigs' feet. I know, the idea of eating pigs' feet might sound a little distasteful to those with delicate tastes, but to me, they were delicious. There were some cousins I recall that wouldn't touch them with a ten-foot pole. But, for Dad and me, they were a tradition—a somewhat messy tradition. You had to split the bones and eat around them, and the process always left me with greasy fingers, but I sat by Dad and ate them every Christmas morning, just like he did.

When it was time for the big Christmas dinner, there were usually so many kids we all got to eat first. The children would sit down at the table to a feast of ham, cured in the smokehouse Grandpa had built—and turkey with all the side dishes, along with figs sent from Aunt Betty. The figs in heavy syrup came in a metal keg from a specialty store in California and always arrived in time for

Christmas dinner. Granny served the figs in a beautiful dish and also added her own homemade spiced peaches in syrup to the table, too. She would also take dates, press a pecan half into each one and roll them in powdered sugar for another treat. All of this, was in addition to her delicious pies and plum pudding. The pudding was made with a hard brandy sauce as icing. One Christmas when Will was in South Africa, he heard Granny Lane was making all the fixins' for Christmas dinner and commented that he "couldn't hardly stand to be away."

Of course, as mentioned in an earlier chapter, we didn't understand it then, but the reason we youngsters got to have an early Christmas dinner was because our folks could then shoo us out to either play outside or, go up to the attic to play, if it was too cold outside. Then, they could sit down to a relaxed meal and grownup conversation, free from distractions that always come when kids are at the table. The adults called it "eating at second table" and I'm sure it was something they looked forward to each Yuletide season.

Understanding Uncle Will's Popularity

I have tried to think long and hard about the impact Uncle Will had on folks. I think it was his simple, honest, yet harmless way of summing up what the majority of people were thinking anyway. He didn't try to use sophisticated terms or philosophical themes, yet he was read by some of the most intelligent, sophisticated audiences in the world. His wit and wisdom was never used in a mean-spirited manner, but in a charming tongue-in-cheek way that had people saying, "You know, Will's got a point."

He had a quick mind but, also, a warm generous heart that somehow came through in everything he said or wrote. Comparatively, I suppose his humor was most like Mark Twain, or later, Bob Hope. Uncle Will's old fashioned sense of morality drew people in to believe in a better, more sensible society. There were many actors, radio stars, newspaper columnists, satirists, humorists, or commentators, but rarely did you see all of the above in one individual. Will Rogers, a plain-spoken man from Oklahoma, spoke for all of America during serious times when folks desperately needed to laugh. If you are up there listening (and I believe you are), "Thanks, Uncle Will."

Granny Lane's Death Hit Us Hard, Especially Uncle Will

> "Death didn't scare her. It was only an episode in her life. If you live right, death is a Joke to you as far as fear is concerned."
>
> —Will Rogers

Before Granny Lane became sick and bed-ridden no one could out-work her. Maud Rogers Lane worked from sun-up to bed time. In my recollection, she seemed to be constantly in motion; working, cooking, cleaning, caring for others. I believe she enjoyed working and took a personal pride in running the farm. Granddad Lane kept busy with the drug store, so, she was in charge of the small dairy operation and was able to make it pay. The extra income paid for the machinery, the hired hands, and then she had money left over for church and other charities. There was even enough left over to buy lovely clothes for her family and herself.

Sometimes Granny would personally drive the wooden, horse-drawn wagon to deliver Sunset Farm milk to neighbors around Chelsea. But, usually that job fell to Monday, the black gentleman who for years was Granny Lane's loyal helper. There were metal racks on the wagon, each with holders for a half-dozen bottles of milk. Monday would put the milk in the racks and then sit up front to drive the horses. Each side of the wagon had a long bench, and Monday would place the bottle holders under the benches to keep the milk from spilling. The Sunset Farm milk wagon was a familiar sight on the streets of Chelsea. Even at my age, I could tell Monday took pride in driving it through town. Other hired help would be necessary in the fall when the hogs and cattle were butchered, or, when the corn, wheat, and alfalfa needed to be harvested.

By early 1925 everyone began to notice that Granny Lane was not as energetic as usual. She complained of an overwhelming tiredness. She was taken to doctors, but none could determine the source of her weakness. When her brother, Will Rogers, whom she had practically raised, heard she was ill, he was deeply concerned. He made a trip from New York back to Chelsea to personally travel with his sister to Mayo's Clinic, saying,

"Maud, I want to take you to Mayo's. They are the best, and they ought to be able to help you."

She underwent a battery of tests at the famous hospital in Rochester, Minnesota, then was sent home with some medication, but nothing seemed to help very much. She kept slowing down, doing less and less around the farm. Then, one day, she suffered a paralyzing stroke, which left her bedfast. Uncle Will hired a registered nurse from Tulsa, fifty miles away, to come and live with us six days a week and provide round-the-clock professional care. He and Aunt Betty also purchased the most up-to-date hospital bed they could find and had it shipped to Sunset Farm.

Even with the extra help, our family became involved in helping Granny Lane everyday. Mimi and I learned to use the crank on the hospital bed to change Granny's position and make her as comfortable as possible. We'd make runs back and forth from the kitchen to the second floor with food and drink for her, and do other little things to assist the nurse.

One of our biggest responsibilities involved answering the door, greeting Granny's guests, and escorting them up to her room. There were two big upholstered armchairs and a wooden straight-back chair, for those who wanted to be a little closer to the bed to visit with Granny. Although ill, Granny always made a point of being nicely dressed; the chest-of-drawers next to the bed was filled with gowns and robes and lacy bed jackets. Her long white hair would always be brushed and pinned up neatly. She was perpetually ready, it seemed, to receive visitors—and there were plenty of them.

I remember how women friends of Granny Lane would get dressed up to pay a call on Granny, wearing straw hats in warm weather, felt hats in cooler months. They arrived, carrying small purses with drawstrings or flat, single-handled purses with fancy closers. Most ladies came to visit carrying plates of cookies or a bouquet of flowers from their gardens. Even back then, many also carried calling cards which they would leave in a tray just inside the entry way. Granny would enjoy looking through the many cards that had collected there.

Just before Christmas that year we moved Granny Lane, her sickbed and all of her furniture, into the Tower room. From there she could see the big tree festooned with the strings of electric colored lights Uncle Will had sent. She would also be able to look out upon the carolers who'd come by from town.

Unable to move much because of her stroke, Granny Lane stayed upbeat, at least as far as the world could see. She never complained and always warmly welcomed her visitors, whether it was the lady from down the road or her famous brother, who would often arrive from halfway across the country to check on her.

Soon after Granny became increasingly ill, the milk business began to dwindle. With Grandpa Lane gone and Granny Lane so ill, it became impossible to maintain. Dad was working nights in the strip mines and had to sleep during the day. Mother was able to tend the garden and the chickens, but her priority was taking care of Granny, so she wasn't able to take over the milking operation and Monday had added responsibilities as well. In just a few months after our move to Sunset Farm, the once small, yet thriving dairy business would come to an end.

On one particular visit toward the end of her life, Uncle Will exited Granny's room with tears beginning to roll down his cheeks. When he was sure he was far enough away that she couldn't hear, he tearfully told me, "Coke, we can't ever let her see us crying. It'd just make her feel bad."

Around the same time, Granny called in her daughter, Aunt Stella, and asked her to go out and by a suit for Monday. She said, "I know he'll want to go to my funeral service and I want him to look nice. I don't want any discrimination. Monday has always helped me and been an important part of my life. He deserves to pay his respects at my service." Granny must have had a strong premonition that her death was imminent—she expressed her wishes for the funeral service and began to say "goodbye" to family and close friends. Aunt Betty, Will's wife, and Granny Lane loved each other very much and Betty came from New York to Sunset Farm to be with Granny during her last days. Uncle Will was fulfilling a busy performance schedule for the *Ziegfeld Follies*, but was getting updates often from Aunt Betty concerning Granny's condition. He'd done everything possible; given his time, money and love to care for the sister who had given so much to him in his childhood. I'm sure his heart was heavy.

Maud Rogers Lane passed away at the age of fifty-six on May 15, 1925, only a year after we lost Granddad. I don't recall specifics of her death. She was taking medicine and I never thought she was in too much pain. There was always someone with her so I'm sure either the nurse or a family member was in the room or close by when she passed away. When Will received word of his sister's death, he immediately left the show in New York and caught a train to Chelsea with the blessings of Ziegfeld himself and the entire cast, which included at the time, W. C. Fields, the popular comedian.

I recall the men from the funeral home coming and taking Granny's body away, only to return her to us in a beautiful casket, dressed up and looking as though she could start talking to us again at any moment. As was the custom, her body was available for viewing in our parlor until the day of the funeral. During those few days, family members received people who seemed to arrive in an unending stream, as they dropped by to pay their respects. Nearly everyone who visited during that period brought in meals and desserts we shared with the many visitors.

The funeral was held at the Chelsea Methodist Church and every pew was filled, some people having to stand in the back. What struck most in attendance that day was the variety of people from every walk of life who came to honor Granny. Of course, Uncle Will and Aunt Betty were there. Then, sitting next to bankers and professional white folk, were Indian relatives and acquaintances, black families whom Granny called 'friends,' and cowboys who had been part of her life as far back as her childhood days on Dog Iron Ranch. The eclectic mix of people shared space in the pews, but more importantly, they shared memories and a deep respect for a wonderful mother and grandmother, a good businesswoman, a woman with a great sense of humor, and a pillar of her community.

The minister had visited Granny on so many occasions and had discussed her wishes for the services including her favorite scripture verses and special hymns to be sung by the choir. Although, surely asked, Uncle Will did not speak at the funeral. He was experiencing a genuine, deep grief and, most likely, was not able or interested in speaking at the service.

Granny was laid to rest in the Chelsea Cemetery next to Granddad. If one were to visit today, they would see a large stone standing six feet tall or more with the family name, Lane, engraved in large letters. Surrounding this massive stone are the individual headstones of deceased family members. In the same cemetery the graves of Clem and Mary Rogers, Will's parents can be located. They both were first buried on a private plot on Dog Iron Ranch in Oologah. However, when the land was flooded in 1961 to create Oologah Lake, the remains of the Rogers family were moved to the Chelsea Cemetery.

The headstone for Granny Lane simply states her name, birth date and date of death. No words could express the impact of a woman who lived such a meaningful, caring, and exuberant life.

A few days following Granny Lane's death and funeral, Uncle Will's weekly column was released. Perhaps his most intimate and beautifully written article, it reflected his pride in his sister and his sadness at her passing. The article revealed a side to the famous humorist that people rarely saw. When I read the article I sense Uncle Will's longing for home and to be around folks he knew and loved; folks that knew and accepted and loved him as well. I have included the entire article below which includes the now famous and heart-warming line: "You can roam all over the World, but after all, it's what the people at home think of you that really counts."

> "A few days ago I was asked by one of the big Ministers of New York City to come to a Luncheon and speak to over 300 Ministers and prominent Laymen. He sat in my dressing room for over an hour. I tried to explain to him that I was only a teller of jokes and that would be all out of tune with the audience he would

have. He is the Methodist Minister here who is building the wonderful big Church (Broadway Temple) which will be the tallest building in New York. A Club, a home, a meeting place, a recreation place for everybody that is interested in trying to live a nice clean wholesome life, and wants to be thrown with people interested in the same thing.

Well, I had worked at affairs for every denomination in the World here in New York, because one is just as worthy as the other. Old New York, the so called heartless city, houses some great people in every denomination in the world, and I can't see any difference in them. I haven't been able to see where one has the monopoly on the right course to Heaven.

I told him I didn't know what to talk about. Saying the erection of this wonderful Church, and worthwhile center, was of course understood as everyone knew that it was a wonderful undertaking. But, anyway, I went and never in my life did I face an audience with as little preparation. Well, I floundered around from one subject to another. The Minister in introducing me had said that I had been raised a Methodist, and I had. So when I got off on that I just couldn't help but speak of a thing which I didn't want to speak of. I knew what would happen if I did.

Out of a large family of which I am the youngest, I have two sisters living (Maud Lane and Sallie McSpadden). And I couldn't speak of any Church without bringing in the work that these two sisters have done, in the little town in which they both live. It's Chelsea, Oklahoma, which means nothing in your life, but it has meant a lot to people who have lived in association with them.

They started in this little Western Town some 35 years ago. They helped build the Methodist Church, the first church there. They have helped every Church, they have helped every movement that they knew was for the best upbuilding of their community. They have each raised a large family of boys and girls who are today a credit to their community. They have carried on the same as thousands of women have carried on in every small and big town in the World. They don't think they are doing anything out of the ordinary. They don't want credit. They do good simply because they don't know any other thing to do.

The reason I spoke of this personal thing is because I couldn't help it. My wife was waiting at the train right then for me to see her off to the sickbed on one of these sisters. I didn't tell this to the Ministers because they are my sisters but because none of them who has given his entire life and time to God could have given any more than they have. They have given their all.

Now when I had finished my little talk to rush to the train to see my wife off, I had something happen that had never happened before and I have spoken at a great many affairs. The entire 300 stood up and offered a Silent Prayer for my poor afflicted sister. That was days ago.

Today, as I write this, I am not in the Follies, the carefree Comedian who jokes about everything. I am out in Oklahoma, among my People, my Cherokee people, who don't expect a laugh for everything I say.

That Silent Prayer that those 300 Ministers uttered didn't save my sister (Maud). She has passed away. But she had lived such a life that it was a privilege to pass away. Death didn't scare her. It was only an episode in her life. If you live right, death is a Joke to you as far as fear is concerned.

And on the day that I am supposed to write a so called Humorous Article I am back home. Back home, at the funeral of my sister. I can't be funny. I don't want to be funny. Even Ziegfeld don't want me to be funny. I told him I wanted to go. He said, 'I would hate you if you didn't.' I told W. C. Fields, the principal comedian of the show. He said, 'Go on, I will do something to fill in.' Brandon Tynan, my friend of years said, 'Go home where you want to be and where you ought to be.'

After all, there is nothing in the world like home. You can roam all over the World, but after all, it's what the people at home think of you that really counts. I have just today witnessed a Funeral that for real sorrow and real affection I don't think will ever be surpassed anywhere. They came in every mode of conveyance, on foot, in Buggies, Horseback, Wagons, Cars, and Trains, and there wasn't a Soul that come that she hadn't helped or favored at one time or another.

> Now, we are in the South, of the South, and according to Northern standards we don't rate the Negro any too high. Well, I wish you could have seen the Negroes at her home on the day of the Funeral. Before her death, she said, 'They are my folks, they have helped me for years, they are all my friends. When I am gone I don't want you Children at my Funeral to show any preference.' That's the real South's real feelings for its real friends. Death knows no Denomination. Death draws no color line.
>
> "Some uninformed Newspapers printed: 'Mrs. C. L. Lane, sister of the famous Comedian, Will Rogers.' They were greatly misinformed. It's the other way around. I am the brother of Mrs. C. L. Lane, "The friend of Humanity." And I want to tell you that as I saw all these people who were there to pay tribute to her memory, it was the proudest moment of my life that I was her brother. And all the honors that I could ever in my wildest dreams hope to reach, would never equal the honor paid on a little western Prairie hilltop, among her people, to Maud Lane. If they will love me like that at the finish, my life will not have been in vain."

Our family continued to live at Sunset Farm until 1929. Giving up Granny Lane's milk business was a gradual process, but finally we just couldn't keep it up. Eventually, the cattle and the farming equipment would be sold, too. Even the little house where Monday and his family lived would soon stand vacant, a sad reminder of happier days when Granny Lane was a dynamic force in all of our lives.

As I read the tribute article written by Uncle Will I realize how much Uncle Will's life was shaped by his sister. Several things stand out to me:

First and foremost, Uncle Will had a profound gratefulness for his sister who had taken him under her wing when his mother died. She became his provider, protector, and mentor. Even his wit and humor could be traced back to the influence of an older sister who took life on and relished it in spite of setbacks or hard times. Like Granny Lane, Uncle Will inherited a respect for all persons, regardless of color or creed. Also, Will's sister taught him that hard work, perseverance, honesty, and kindness were words to live by. Finally, it surely was Granny Lane who impressed upon Will the importance of family and friendship. I can almost hear her speaking the words that Uncle Will wrote, " ... it's what the people at home think of you that really counts."

Even though I was young when she passed away, I would miss so many things about Granny Lane. My life, too, was greatly influenced and shaped by a strong, hardworking, unselfish Oklahoma woman who raised great children, among them a brother who would be known around the world and a wonderful son; my father.

Uncle Will's Generous Heart

> "It's great to be great, but it's greater to be human."
>
> —Will Rogers

In 1924, the typical yearly income for a middle class American family was around $1,260. That doesn't sound like much, but a loaf of bread was only 9 cents and milk could be purchased for 13 cents a gallon. A family could get a new car for around $300 and a new home cost about $5,000. In comparison, you might say Uncle Will was making very good money from the early 1900's on. During the final days of his vaudeville performances he made nearly $500 a week. Hollywood wanted him for the film business in 1918, and offered a salary that was staggering to most people at the time, and would be impressive still today. By 1929, during the Depression, Fox Films guaranteed Will a weekly salary of around $13,000. On top of that he would receive $150,000 to $187,000 for each film produced. He was scheduled for six pictures in 86 weeks which means Uncle Will earned more than $1,000,000 that year alone! Of course, he starred in many more films and that doesn't take into account compensation for his radio performances or the syndicated newspaper column written weekly.

There were several signs that Uncle Will was doing well. In 1920, he purchased 186 acres in Santa Monica, California, overlooking the Pacific Ocean, now known as Pacific Palisades. His dream was to recreate his Oklahoma ranch as much as possible; and he did so, on a much grander scale. At the time of his death in 1935 the ranch consisted of the 31 room ranch house, corral and stables, riding and roping arenas, swimming pool, a polo field, a golf course and winding hiking trails all around the beach front property. When Aunt Betty passed away in 1944, the property became part of California's state park system and is visited by thousands each year.

For all of the wealth he was accumulating, Uncle Will remained frugal and careful about spending, but extremely generous to those in need. He began to consider the requests from many charitable institutions and programs.

Even before he was wealthy, Will would send money home to Grandpa Rogers for various needs around the home place and he also tried to save as much money as possible, banking most of his earnings. One of the most meaningful gifts from Uncle Will was sent to Aunt Betty after she finally agreed to be his wife. It was a small lace handkerchief he purchased years before from an old woman he met while in South Africa. When he bought the handkerchief, the lady asked if he was married. He told her he wasn't, then she told him to give the handkerchief to the woman he would marry someday. He had been saving the handkerchief for a special someone. He carried it with him through South Africa, through Australia, and then home, always intending to do as the old woman said. Aunt Betty treasured that small lace handkerchief.

Matching Buicks and a Horse Named, 'Streaky'

Not long after Granddad Lane passed away and just before our family moved to Sunset Farm, Uncle Will purchased two new matching Buick Sedans for both of his sisters, Aunt Sally McSpadden and my grandmother, Maud Lane. At the time, in 1924, he was still in New York appearing in the *Ziegfeld Follies* and had also spent several months in Hollywood making a series of two-reel comedies for producer, Hal Roach. Already famous, Will was also writing his weekly column by then. This generous gesture to his sisters was indicative of how he never forgot the folks back home in Oklahoma and showed his appreciation to family members who had given so much to him.

Following our move to Sunset Farm we received another surprise gift from Uncle Will. One afternoon a truck pulled up into the driveway and a man we did not know, hopped out of the truck, came to the door and motioned toward the truck and said, "I'm delivering a pony for Will Rogers. He says it's for the kids."

We all stood around the truck while the driver carefully unloaded a beautiful black pony, with a white stripe down its nose. Even Dad seemed to be totally surprised by the gift. The kids were elated and quickly led the pony to the barn where we made a stall for him, and, just like that, "Streaky" came to be a part of our family. It didn't take long for us to name him, referencing the dominant streak of white on the horse's nose.

Horses had always been an important part of Uncle Will's life while growing up on the family ranch near Oologah. Before he could even sit up, he was riding on horses with his father. By the time he was a toddler, he had been given his own pony. He used to tell us kids something his father, Clem Rogers had told him, "Always ride your own horse;" a small bit of wisdom Grandpa Rogers probably heard from his father, Robert Rogers. Undoubtedly, Uncle Will enjoyed horses in his childhood and wanted us to have one, too. Whatever the reason, we were thrilled with the pony. Soon Mimi, and Bob and I, were riding Streaky single and double all around the farm.

Because we were too small to get up on Streaky's back very easily, we would lead him down to a big catalpa tree that grew in the yard, then climb up in the branches and jump down onto the saddle. If the horse minded the unorthodox way of mounting up, we didn't know it. He remained remarkably good-natured even with three rowdy young owners.

Mother kept us all in line, though—even Streaky. When she wanted us to come in, or needed us for something, she would whistle. She was good at it, too. No matter where we were on the farm, we could always hear her. And, after Streaky had been with us for a while, he'd take off for the house himself every time he heard Mother whistle.

Uncle Will Loved Giving at Christmas

Uncle Will's generous nature was always apparent at Christmas time. As mentioned previously, it was well-known by the family that Uncle Will, like many men, was a last minute shopper. He did not do his Christmas shopping for his immediate family until Christmas Eve. In the book, *Will Rogers: His Wife's Story* written by Aunt Betty, she tells how he would go out shopping "usually the day before Christmas." He would remember everyone who worked for or with him, then he would come home with "mountains of toys and clothing" for his family and spend Christmas Eve wrapping gifts.

Often on Christmas Day, the family would retreat to a little log cabin on their California property, where they could spend the day in seclusion. The children took turns at being Santa. Once when it was Mary's turn, their daughter fixed up her pony with Christmas trappings, packed a sack and rode the pony right into the house. Only once after his marriage was Will away from his wife and children at Christmas, but he sent gifts home that year, 1931, and spent a lonely Christmas in Shanghai.

Although Uncle Will never made it back home to Oklahoma for Christmas after I was born, I remember well the gifts he sent home for the family.

Electric Lights and Checks to Folks Back Home

We had some of the first electric Christmas lights ever seen in Chelsea because Uncle Will sent them to us from New York during the first Christmas we spent on Sunset Farm. No one in Chelsea had ever even heard of lights on trees. Candles were often used back then to light a tree, but could be extremely dangerous. So, when we received the lights it was a special treat. Dad helped Monday place them on the big cedar tree at the end of the lane and, to us, the sight was breathtaking. You may recall that we moved Granny Lane to the tower room specifically so that she could view the lights on the tree from her window.

Carolers would come out to the farm and stand beneath Granny's window to sing the carols that Granny loved to hear. We helped mother fill sacks with oranges and candy to give to each caroler who visited.

Uncle Will consistently showed his love for his family back in Oklahoma by sending personal checks to all the family at Christmas. I have kept a copy of a Christmas letter sent from Uncle Will to Mother and Dad from Beverly Hills on December 22, 1932. The envelope contained checks for the whole family.

"I GUESS YOU ALL WILL GO DOWN TO STELLS FOR XMAS," he wrote in the body of the letter, which was typed in all capital letters and contained vintage Will Rogers spelling, syntax, and turns of phrase. Here are some other excerpts:

"IS HAP AND LASKA, AND DARN IT I CANT FOR THE SAKE OF ME TONIGHT THINK OF HAPS NAME, SO YOU TELL LASKA TO FILL OUT THIS CHECK IN HER NAME, IF SHE CAN REMEMBER IT. I KNOW THE HAP PART ALLRIGHT, BUT YOU GOT TO BE A POLITICIAN TO REMEMBER ALL THE NAMES.

I DON'T KNOW HOW TO REACH THEM SO WILL SEND ALL OF THEM TO YOU, SO DON'T GOBBLE ONTO THE WHOLE BUNCH, I DON'T KNOW STELLS HOUSE ADDRESS IN TULSA EITHER. TELL EM ALL TO GET THEIR

CHILDREN SOMETHING WITH PART OF THIS AND ITS FROM ME TO THEM. I WOULD LIKE TOO SEE EM ALL, AND WILL SOME TIME, AS I WILL BE PASSING THROUGH AND MABY CAN STOP LONGER ... MUCH LOVE TO ALL OF YOU AND ALL THE CHILDREN. UNCLE WILL."

As we grew older, Uncle Will would send us Christmas checks made payable to us personally. I don't recall hearing Dad and Mother speak about the amount of the checks Uncle Will sent, but it was a substantial amount and always very much appreciated by all the kinfolk. Most were struggling to make ends meet, especially during the years of the Great Depression. Oklahoma was one of the hardest-hit states and I'm sure the extra money from Uncle Will was a much-welcomed blessing.

I remember specifically spending my part of the money Uncle Will sent for a new pair of shoes. Then, the family would pool the rest for a big summer vacation, usually spent visiting relatives in Texas and New Mexico.

A Fire Destroyed the Lane Home, but Not Their Spirit

Uncle Will saw that his good fortune could benefit others in need. This had always been the case even before he and Aunt Betty became wealthy. When they married, the couple started putting a dollar a day into a strong box that traveled with them from town to town. Once out on the road, they arrived at the hotel where they would be staying, a while after their baggage had been delivered. The strongbox had been broken into and rifled through. Their savings, amounting to $125.00 had disappeared along with Aunt Betty's jewelry. The money represented a great deal of sacrifice on their part, but Uncle Will was philosophical about it. "Well, Betty," he said, "at least we're not as bad off as Maud was. Her whole house burnt down."

He was referring to the fire of 1903 that completely destroyed his sister's home. When the house burned to the ground, Uncle Will was not in a financial position to help much, as his career had only begun. Granddad Lane started rebuilding the home, but the tragic fire and aftermath impacted Uncle Will, because he spoke of it often. For years, while on tour he referred to the loss his sister and family experienced mentioning how they escaped with only the clothes on their backs. He was impressed with the resilient spirit of his sister even while she and her family were dependent on the community. For weeks, the Lanes went to church wearing clothes donated to them by friends around Chelsea.

Uncle Will's Desire to Give Was Born Out of Deep Loss

Aunt Betty once spoke to me personally and offered her insight into why providing for and giving to his family was important to Uncle Will. Losing his mother when he was only ten years old had a profound impact upon Will and had a great deal to do with his expressed love and generosity toward us. "When his mother died," Aunt Betty said, "he was kind of lost. He seemed to be always trying to make up for something that was missing in his own life. He never got over his mother's death."

His own personal loss made Will especially sensitive to the needs of children and charities that supported children's causes.

He Gave to Those Going Through Hard Times—He Knew What That Was Like

Whenever anyone needed a little cash, Uncle Will's hand was first to reach into his pocket. He was what they call, "a soft touch." People would wait for him out on the street by Fox's studio gates, many of them old cowboys trying to make a living in Hollywood working in western movies. They'd say, "Why, Will, you remember me? I worked with you at the X-I-T Ranch (or some other place and time)." He would give them a few bills, along with a pat on the back and some words of encouragement.

"This will tide you over for today," he'd say, "and things'll get better tomorrow."

Uncle Will's generosity didn't just extend to individuals. In the early '30's, when the one-two punch of the Great Depression and the Dust Bowl were pounding Oklahoma, Uncle will visited the state on a tour designed to raise money for those hit hardest. Will would do many benefit shows and donate all the money to the Red Cross or Salvation Army, and when the basket was passed, he wrote the first check.

I remember Aunt Betty telling my sister, Mimi and I that she and Will never had a fuss over money in their whole married lives, despite his tendency to give what he had away. "I can't explain it, girls," she said. "He just wants to give and give."

From their earliest hardscrabble days out on the vaudeville circuit, Aunt Betty always took care of the finances. She hardly ever talked about money to us kids, but I remember her telling how, after Uncle Will became a movie star, she would put cash out on the dresser at the ranch, so he'd always have some "walking-around" money on him. He'd pick the money up each morning; put it in his pocket, and head off, usually to the Fox studios, where he was appearing in pictures at that time. Invariably, she said, he'd return home without a dime.

So, she'd put more out on the dresser each morning, and still he'd come back each evening with empty pockets. "Finally," she said, "I asked him where he was spending all that money."

"Well, Betty, I ran into an old fella from Oklahoma who was down on his luck. He needed gas to get to a job. Then, one of the girls at the studio needed an operation, and everybody took up a collection."

Aunt Betty knew Uncle Will would give the coat off his back if someone needed it. It was just part of his character that would be spoken of and admired by all.

During one of the early trips Will made to Bartlesville, he visited with his good friend Frank Phillips, the famed oilman, about the problems the country, and in particular, Oklahoma, was having due to the Depression. Mr. Phillips wondered what else could be done to help. He expressed to Will that everyone in his company, from the top executive to the janitor, had taken a five-percent pay cut to prevent layoffs.

Mr. Phillips was considering other ways by which he could help the folks around his hometown of Bartlesville.

At this time, our family had moved from Sunset Farm into Bartlesville and it was my dad who visited with Uncle Will and Mr. Phillips and offered a tangible suggestion. "You know, all the churches have large indebtedness because we got carried away with building in the late '20's, when there was plenty of money around. Now, people can't afford the pledges they made and the bank notes are not being met."

So, Mr. Phillips agreed to pay off the notes of all the Bartlesville churches. Just about the only congregation that hadn't accumulated debt was the Baptist group, because they had paid as they went. But he gave them a nice amount, too, just to keep things even among all the churches.

A Special Women's Club Receives a Gift From Uncle Will Just Before His Death

In 1935, just months before Uncle Will's fated Alaska trip, he was visiting with one of his sisters, my aunt, Sallie McSpadden. She mentioned during the visit that the volunteer club she was part of had a special need. The General Federation of Womens' Clubs was a prominent international organization at the time headquartered in Washington, D. C. More than two million members from thirty-three countries made up the largest volunteer group in the world. The president of Oklahoma's chapter was Roberta Campbell Lawson, granddaughter of Charles Journeycake, the last chief of the Delaware tribe. Roberta was a northeastern Oklahoma girl, born in Alluwe and living in Nowata, Oklahoma. Her husband worked in the oil business in Tulsa, so they also had a beautiful home there as well.

Aunt Sallie shared with Will that the General Federation was having its convention in Detroit that year, and all the clubwomen in Oklahoma were working toward the goal of making Roberta president of the entire organization. "But," she said to Will, "it probably won't happen because we don't have enough support to get our Oklahoma delegation to the convention."

"I know Roberta," Will responded. "She'd be perfect for that. What would you need to register your delegation?"

Aunt Sallie told him it would cost about $500.

"Well, you get your delegation together," said Will. "I'll give you the money."

Included in that group was my mother, who traveled to Detroit as a representative of the Tuesday Club of Bartlesville, Oklahoma. I remember her buying a real pretty blue suit to wear to the convention. Aunt Sallie also made the trip, along with other ladies from Chelsea's Delphian Review Club, which Mother also belonged to.

Upon arriving at the convention, the whole state delegation began campaigning hard to let everyone know about Roberta and her desire to be the international president. Their work paid off. Roberta Campbell won her bid to become president and Uncle Will was very pleased about the outcome. He knew Roberta would represent Oklahoma and her native American people well on a worldwide stage. (She represented not only the Delaware tribe, but the Cherokee people too, since the Delawares were also adopted Cherokees.)

When the ladies made their triumphant return from Michigan, there was no way any of them would have dreamed that their famous benefactor, Will Rogers would be dead within a couple of months. In fact, out of the huge number of obituaries written in honor of Uncle Will, many mentioned that one of the last things he had done was to help get a group of Oklahoma women to the General Federation of Women' Clubs Convention in Detroit. Mother wore the blue suit she'd purchased for the Convention to Uncle Will's funeral.

This book could not contain all the many personal stories we have heard and read about Uncle Will's generosity. I especially love something that Uncle Will said, "That's one trouble with our charities, we are always saving somebody away off, when the fellow next to us ain't eating." Our family experienced Will's caring heart again and again. I hope he knew how his many gifts, like the string of electric lights on Christmas, made our lives brighter and richer in ways that will live in my memory for as long as I live.

Leaving Sunset Farm: Our Move to Bartlesville

> "Oklahoma is the heart, it's the vital organ, of our national existence."
>
> —Will Rogers

Memories of riding Streaky across the open pastures of Sunset Farm, carefree childish laughter trailing behind us into the gold-laced sunset of a rural Oklahoma day, remain vivid. The years spent there, living with Granny Lane in her grand house in Chelsea, provide me with some of my dearest memories. So, it is with great sadness whenever I recall the circumstances by which our family had to leave Sunset Farm.

It seems that several events collided all at once during and just following the death of Granny Lane in 1925. Her death, in and of itself, was quite a shock as she had remained active and full of vitality until the last year of her life. Granddad and Granny Lane passing away only months apart was difficult for the entire Rogers clan. At the same time, the country was beginning to wind down from the wild spending flapper era and would soon reap the results of reckless overindulgence. The Great Depression wreaked havoc across the nation after the stock market crash of 1929, but seemed worse here in the Midwest, because it coincided with severe drought. While tycoons who lost millions in the crash jumped to their death from Wall Street windows, the Dust Bowl in Oklahoma caused hundreds to pack up and migrate west to hopefully find work. John Steinbeck's novel, *The Grapes of Wrath* depicted the plight of "Okies" who left the state during this time when the relentless dust buried homes, killed cattle, and devastated crops. Many were forced to move, but they left their hearts right here on the Oklahoma plains and hoped to return.

True to it's name, the Great Depression was a depressing time for most Americans. Parents were struggling to feed their families and provide other bare necessities. My siblings and I didn't understand the reasons behind so many being out of work and impoverished. All we knew was that in 1929 it became apparent that Dad and his sisters were going to have to sell Sunset Farm and we were told the family would be moving to Bartlesville, fifty miles away from the place we had known and loved all of our lives.

Preparing to Leave the Farm

It was late summer in 1929 when Sunset Farm was sold to a family by the name of Goff. There were many things we needed to do before handing over the place. General clean up was underway and Dad was making sure repairs were made around the farm. One of the biggest tasks I was assigned was to help Mimi carry mounds of newspapers and old magazines all the way from the top attic room outside to be burned. I think Granddad Lane must have kept every National Geographic Magazine in existence. Then, there were also dozens of copies of Colliers and Harper's Weekly magazines my grandmother had saved. Mother watched and managed the fire outside as we carried down tons of paper from the attic to be burned.

I don't recall the details of leaving our horse, Streaky. I am most inclined to believe we sold the pony, too, knowing we would not have a place for the horse in Bartlesville. I am reminded of something Uncle Will said. "A man that don't love a horse, there is something the matter with him." Our family agreed; we loved that horse.

512 South Chickasaw, Bartlesville, Oklahoma

Dad took a job as a clerk at National Supply Company in Bartlesville. National sold oilfield supplies to the related companies in and around the area of the once thriving oil town. Aunt Stella, Dad's sister, was married to James Neal who was the company's treasurer, so word of the job opening came from him.

Our first home in Bartlesville was a nice, two-story, three bedroom rent house at 512 South Chickasaw in Bartlesville. We were settling in and getting involved with school when the bottom fell out of the economy and National had to lay many off. Dad, being one of the most recent hires, was one of the first to go. He had to scramble to find other work in those hard times. For a couple of years following, he worked selling Ford automobiles for a dealership owned by a gentleman by the name of Burt Gaddis. However, as you can imagine, not many people could afford new cars during this period, so he had a very hard time, but I'm sure he learned a lot from the experience.

We lived in the house on South Chickasaw for a year before we moved to 416 W. 4th, a house which backed up to an alley way directly across from Jefferson Elementary School located at 4th and Choctaw. Mimi was in the 5th grade and I was in the 4th. Bob and Jane, our younger siblings were in the 2nd and 1st grade at Jefferson as well. Our younger sister, Maude Estelle, whom we called, "Pudge" was too young for school at this point. Mother told the story about attending a parents meeting at Jefferson for the new school year. Parents were asked to stand if they had a child who would be enrolled in the first grade, the second grade, and so on. Mother stood up so many times, a lady next to her, thinking Mother misunderstood the directive, said, "Mrs. Lane, you just need to stand up only for your child's particular grade."

She responded, "I am. I happen to have a child in almost every grade!"

I have four lifelong friends from this period in Bartlesville. In fact, our group of friends called ourselves "The 4th street gang." We were constantly in each other's homes and finding fun and adventure whenever together. The "gang" frequented Webster's Grocery Store nearby and in the summer played outdoors until dark each day. We remained close through our junior high and high school years at Bartlesville Central.

Finally, Dad landed a full-time job as a supervisor at the Farm Security Administration (FSA), one of the many "alphabet soup" agencies that newly elected

President Franklin Roosevelt had created to try and combat wide-spread unemployment and deal with the effects of the Depression. Dad would talk to farmers and ranchers and do his best to help them get government loans, because at that time they were losing everything they had. I recall how disturbed Dad would become about the government requiring ranchers to kill their livestock in order to keep prices up. The ranchers were not allowed to give the animals away even for the purpose of feeding hungry people, because it would drive the market down. So, at the behest of the government cattlemen were shooting their cattle and burying them. It was the toughest of times for everyone.

Uncle Will's Special Visits

Well before Dad took the government job, he was making regular trips to Tulsa, forty-five miles south of Bartlesville, to meet Uncle Will who usually came into the airport in a passenger plane. Dad would drive to pick him up in one of Burt Gaddis's Fords and then drive Will wherever he wanted to go. Mimi and I would sometimes get to make the trip to Tulsa, too. We'd all sit and visit in the airport manager's office until Uncle Will arrived.

Uncle Will always arrived wearing a suit and hat. Usually he wore a double breasted suit coat, a starched shirt, and at times, depending on the weather, carried an overcoat. He also toted around a portable typewriter in a case. After loading his luggage into the car, Will was patient and kind as he answered the many questions we had. He would tell us about his travels and projects he was working on. He was fun and willing to indulge our curiosity all the way to his destination.

Will seemed very interested in Dad's job with the FSA, so they would often talk about the plight of farmers and ranchers during the drive from the airport. Sports and politics were also frequent subjects for them to toss around.

Uncle Will loved to catch up with relatives and friends when he came home to visit. There were times he wanted to be taken directly from the airport to Chelsea, where he would often congregate with other family members at his sister, Sallie McSpadden's home. Other times he would want to be taken to the family ranch in Oologah. Usually, his northeastern Oklahoma travels would include a stop at my Aunt Estelle's Tulsa home. Dad's sister, Estelle, or, Stella, as we called her, was the oldest child in the Lane family and Uncle Will knew her best, so he enjoyed visiting with her especially whenever he made it back to Oklahoma. As noted earlier, Stella was married to James Neal, the oil-supply executive.

On most occasions upon arriving with Will at Aunt Stella's home, a good meal would be waiting for us. We would eat and then while the adults conversed in the living room, we played with our cousins, Jim and Betty Maude Neal, who were close to our own ages. Sometimes, other young cousins were around as well, especially Harvey Capp Luckett, the son of my dad's youngest sister, Aunt Lasca, (nicknamed 'Winky'). Aunt Sallie McSpadden had grandchildren as well, and many times they would be present at the get-togethers, too. Cousins Clem and Bob McSpadden, and Tom Milan, another cousin about our age, were often there. Some cousins living in Chicago and St. Louis were too far away to be included.

Ice Cream with Uncle Will

At some point, during these visits, Uncle Will would take his battered old portable typewriter out of its case, walk down and set it on Aunt Stella's desk in the hall, then sit down to knock out his daily syndicated column. He wrote the words that would be read by millions of people from Stella's hallway in Tulsa, as we played nearby in another room.

I'm sure we got noisy, but Uncle Will didn't seem to be bothered, nor was he distracted by the grownups visiting. He used only two fingers on the keyboard of the typewriter and just went right on pecking out his "Will Rogers Says" column, oblivious to everything going on around him. We kids would keep an eye on him, however, because we knew what was coming when Uncle Will finished writing.

"C'm'on, Gunter," he'd finally say, getting up and removing the paper, then closing the typewriter case. "Get the kids. We need to get this thing off."

That meant they'd be heading to the Western Union office in Tulsa, where Uncle Will would send off the syndicated column which would be distributed to hundreds of newspapers. At the signal, we'd run out, pile into the Ford, the smaller kids sitting on the laps of the bigger kids, and away we'd go with Dad at the wheel and Uncle Will beside him up front.

Now, going to the telegraph office wasn't a particular treat, even though any ride with Uncle Will was a fun time. But the real fun came after the column was sent. Not far from the Western Union office was an ice cream parlor where Uncle Will would treat everyone to sundaes, or ice cream cones.

We were usually so excited, that it sometimes took a while for each of us kids to make up our minds about what to order. So, Will and Dad would get their sundaes first, then sit down, watching us pore over the possible selections. After we had made our choices and were served, we'd carry our ice cream to a nearby table and chatter away as we enjoyed the special treat. I recall vividly catching a glimpse of Uncle Will watching us with a big smile on his face. He loved ice cream, too.

Will's Hankerin' for Oklahoma Food

In addition to ice cream, Uncle Will was very fond of several other kinds of food, including ham with gravy and steak, as long as it was well done. He especially favored ham that had been cured by his brother-in-law, Tom McSpadden. Uncle Tom butchered beef and hogs, and he and Aunt Sallie always kept plenty of chickens and always had a nice garden, too. Perhaps, it had a lot to do with Will's days as a cowboy, but his top two favorite dishes included beans. He loved soupy ham and beans with cornpone or Oklahoma-made cornbread, and he was also a huge fan of chili; with plenty of beans. In one article he wrote: "Going to have beans for supper tonight … navy beans cooked in Oklahoma ham, raised on the Dog Iron Ranch at Oologah, cooked plenty soupy like. Got to eat 'em with a spoon, raw onions and cornbread, nothing else.

Anybody that would want anything else ought to be shot." Most often, Will was more interested in another helping of beans and cornbread rather than dessert. He bragged on Madelyn McSpadden's beans especially. It seemed that Madelyn, Aunt Sallies' daughter-in-law married to Herb, could cook beans just right. Will commented how unusual it was that "a city girl" like Madelyn could hold her own and cook as well or better than any of the other home-grown gals on the ranch. Herb and Madelyn had two boys, Clem and Bob, already mentioned, then Trent was born later in 1935, a week or two before Uncle Will's ill fated Alaska trip.

Uncle Will once told us that whenever he had a speaking engagement that included a dinner, he would try to sneak into town early and go to a local café, where he'd order a bowl of chili or beans with cornbread and talk to the locals before going to his engagement. That way, he'd have a favorite meal and could visit with the people seated at the head table at the banquet instead of eating the dried chicken and green peas often served at the functions.

Uncle Will Was a Hit with the Neighbor Kids

On one particular visit Will made to our house on Chickasaw in the early '30's, Dad picked him up around noon, so they headed home where Mother had his favorite kind of chili waiting for lunch. After the meal, Dad was to take Uncle Will downtown where he would meet with city leaders and oil people, including his friend, oilman Frank Phillips. Later, Will spent the night at the Phillips' Woolaroc Ranch retreat.

Exiting the house for the drive downtown with Will, we were surprised to see all the kids in the neighborhood standing all over our yard, hoping to catch a glimpse of our famous relative. I'm still not sure how word got out that he was there, but the news of his visit had spread like a prairie fire, and lots of childish faces looked on in awe, wanting to see this real-life movie and radio star.

Uncle Will could've simply grinned and waved, got into the car and drove away. After all, there were important people awaiting him downtown, but that would not have been like Uncle Will. Instead of rushing away, he approached every one of those kids, shaking their hands, offering each a personal word.

A few days later, Mother got a call.

"Mrs. Lane," said the woman. "I hate to bother you, but I can't get my son to wash his hands, because he shook hands with Will Rogers at your house."

She had to assure the young man of Will's return in the future and he'd have another opportunity to shake that famous hand.

The Early '30's in Bartlesville

Our family's move to Bartlesville coincided with the time of Uncle Will's greatest fame. On a more personal note, I was making friends, enjoying school and doing the normal things any young pre-teen girl would do. Entering Bartlesville Junior High School in the seventh grade I was a pretty good athlete. I played basketball and did well in most of my school subjects, but struggled with math. I hated sewing, which most girls enjoyed during that time;

however, I loved to cook. Dad had taught me how to make gravy when I was very young. He especially loved steak with gravy and bragged on my gravy often.

Our family had always been active in church. In Bartlesville, we attended the First United Methodist Church at 5th and Johnstone. We had many "church friends" and I enjoyed Sunday School and Bible study very much.

One interesting note here is that Uncle Will's family, as mentioned, had Methodist roots, as well. In fact, when Will was a youngster, his mother was the pianist for the local church in Oologah. Often the Rogers would have the pastor and his family over for dinner following Sunday services. Will's mother had a piano in their home at Dog Iron Ranch which had been purchased and ordered from Europe, then shipped to New Orleans. From there, it was delivered to the ranch by overland wagon. The piano remains in Will's boyhood Oologah home, which is today a museum. I am certain that his mother's appreciation and love for music was passed on to Uncle Will.

In 1934 our family made another move in Bartlesville to a two story home located at 707 Osage. It had a sleeping porch much like the Sunset Farm home, but the porch was glassed in. We were living in this house in August of 1935, just before my junior year in high school, when word came of the airplane accident which took Uncle Will's life.

Will Rogers: A "Friend of Aviation"

> "I got the real kick of my life out of aviation today. Left western Kansas and flew down to Oklahoma and landed right on the old ranch I was born on. First machine was ever in there. When I was raised here, I never thought there would be anything faster than a horse get in there ..."
>
> —Will Rogers

Uncle Will's love for flying has become legendary. I remember meeting him at the Tulsa airport when he would come in on a commercial flight. However, when he was short on time, and that was most of the time, he would hire a pilot to fly him home in a private plane. He was even flying around Europe before airline passenger service became a reality in the United States.

As far as I know, Will never expressed an interest in becoming a pilot himself, but he sure admired the pilots he came to know. I believe his love for flying came after a memorable flight with General Billy Mitchell, the World War I Brigadier General. Mitchell believed strongly that America needed to develop a strong air force for defensive and military purposes. Uncle Will saw air travel as the wave of the future and agreed wholeheartedly. Later, Will would also fly with Charles Lindbergh and navigator, Harold Gatty, but of course, would become a special friend to a pilot who had Oklahoma roots: Wiley Post.

Wiley Post was born in Grand Saline, Texas, but raised near Maysville, Oklahoma. He lost an eye in an oil field accident in 1924 and used the insurance money received from the accident to purchase his first plane. Wiley and Will established an on-going friendship after Wiley flew Will to an appearance at a rodeo. Wiley became one of the best pilots in the country and gained worldwide fame after he became the first to fly solo around the world in 1931. Post, along with his navigator for the trip, Harold Gatty, was named an aviation hero, visited the White House, and was treated to a ticker-tape parade in New York City.

Wiley was extremely dedicated to inventing methods and developing gear that would allow pilots to fly at ever increasing high altitudes. He is credited with inventing the first air-pressure suit, which, even its crude state, looked similar to what modern day astronauts wear today.

I only saw Wiley Post from a distance. He was a quiet, unassuming man who was comfortable in the background. Sometimes he wore the eye-patch seen in most photos; at other times he would not wear the patch. Usually when he flew Uncle Will in to local airports, Post would dismount the plane and stand around unobtrusively until Will was deposited and met by family. I am sure he was invited to our homes to stay overnight or for dinner, but I never recall him accepting the offer. Of course, it was Wiley Post who asked Uncle Will to accompany him on the tour to

Alaska in 1935 that took both of their lives. Wiley Post was only thirty-six years old at the time of his death.

A Matter of Convenience

As Uncle Will's fame grew in the late 1920's, he was traveling more and more, doing a lot of lecturing across the country. The traveling was often time-consuming and the ability to hire private pilots who could fly him into the next town on the schedule cut the time in half and was less taxing physically.

One family story recounts how Uncle Will once returned home to California via a mail carrier. When he arrived, his youngest son, Jimmy, noticed that his flight jacket was covered with stamps.

"What are all of those for, Dad?" Jimmy asked.

"That's how much the flight cost this time," said Will.

As I understand it, Will had permits to fly on both military and mail planes. So, when he took the latter, he would weigh himself, his jacket or overcoat and his typewriter then pay the postage charge for the combined weight.

Aunt Betty, Will's wife, did not share her husband's passion for flying. In fact, her first flight with him wasn't even in America. Will traveled to Europe in 1926, along with a Hollywood cameraman to record the visit in a series of short films, previously mentioned. Aunt Betty went over to England by ship to join him. Then, she discovered she and Will were scheduled to fly from there across the English Channel to France.

I recall Aunt Betty relating that she'd never thought about wanting to fly, and when the time came to board the plane, she kept hoping the famous London fog would be too thick for take-off. But, it wasn't.

As the plane taxied down the runway, she asked if she could hold Will's hand.

"Why?" he asked, in his typically joking manner. "I wouldn't be any help to you."

Although she white-knuckled that first trip, she quickly determined it wasn't so bad after all. Even in those days, Europe had good commercial aircraft, and whenever she and Uncle Will traveled she had no trouble going by air. Later, she began flying in American passenger planes, over the country that she and Will had crisscrossed by train many times during his vaudeville days. She told us she finally grew to tolerate it.

Still, whenever they had to fly to a destination, Aunt Betty and Uncle Will would intentionally book different flights. The thinking was that should the unthinkable happen and one of the planes went down, the children wouldn't be left by themselves. There was a part of her that remained squeamish about flying, which led to her anxiety about Will's last flight in 1935.

Undressing a Wonderful Oklahoma Woman!

Uncle Will flew in for a memorable event I recall specifically. One evening my dad got a surprise call from Uncle Will.

"This is a secret, Gunter," Will told him. "I'm going to Ponca City for the dedication of a statue, even though I told them I couldn't come because I was in the middle of a picture. So, I don't want them (meaning, the dedication committee) to know I'm going to be there."

Dad understood and agreed to pick Will up at the Tulsa airport on the morning of April 22, 1930, the same day the statue was to be unveiled to the public. Mimi and I got to go with Dad to pick up Uncle Will, and later on, accompanied him to the grand event itself.

The creation of the beautiful statue titled, The Pioneer Woman, to be erected in Ponca City, Oklahoma, had been in the works for four years. The statue depicts a strong, confident woman striding, holding a Bible in one hand, the hand of her son in the other, bonneted head held high, gazing toward the southwest. Planning for the statue began in 1926 when oilman E. W. Marland, commissioned the statue to honor the pioneer women of America. Marland would become governor of Oklahoma in 1935. The statue was to be placed in his hometown of Ponca City. Mr. Marland and Uncle Will had known each other and been friends for several years.

A dozen of the world's most prominent sculptors submitted models for the statue and were given $10,000 each for their efforts. The models were exhibited across the country and people were asked to vote for their favorite. After three-quarters of a million votes were tabulated, the winning creation turned out to be that of British sculptor, Bryant Baker. Baker then created the full-sized statue and received an extra $100,000 from Marland for his efforts.

Once we had Uncle Will and were on our way to Ponca City, Will began to tell us about his recent trip to China. He spoke of his all-day visit to a real Chinese theater.

"We sat on mats on the floor, and they kept bringing courses of food for us to eat with our hands," he said. "When you were finished with each dish, why, you'd just hold your hand up and they'd throw a hot, wet towel to you."

He couldn't tell us the names of the dishes he'd eaten; only that some were good, some weren't, and some were spicy hot. He also said that he really didn't understand the play, but that the dancers were small and graceful and their costumes were very colorful.

By the time we got within a few miles of the dedication site in Ponca City, the streets were teeming with cars and people. The men assigned to traffic control would hold up their hands to stop us and Dad would tell them, "I've got Will Rogers with me, and he's got to get to the platform."

One look in the Ford would verify that our father was telling the truth and they would wave us through the ever-growing crowd. Once we were close enough, Uncle Will hopped form the car and motioned to us,

"Come on girls," he said, taking us by the hands. We had been told to never cling to Uncle Will or try to monopolize his time when he was home. We knew many other people wanted to visit with him and we could always visit with him later. However, this occasion was different: he had invited us to accompany him. So we walked with him to the platform, sticking very close to Uncle Will.

To this day, I remember how happy the dignitaries looked when they first spied Uncle Will climbing onto the stage. They may have been surprised at his presence, but were more than delighted. The crowd, estimated at more than forty-thousand, was delighted to see him, too.

At the moment of the unveiling, when the covering slipped down to reveal the statue, Uncle Will commented, into the microphone, "Oh, this is a wonderful Oklahoma woman, but I never undressed a lady in public before and I never saw a cleaner face on a boy in Oklahoma."

The crowd roared, and as Mimi and I watched our famous uncle, he spoke off the cuff, as usual, about the event and the statue. Tens of thousands of people hung on his every word and we were once again very proud to be related to this man who was loved and respected by so many.

After the festivities were over and Uncle Will had visited with many and shaken the hands of hundreds of people, Mr. Marland invited him to his mansion. We went along with Uncle Will and Dad to the grand home noticing first the ladies at the front door assigned to make sure only certain people gained entrance. The women greeted us warmly and made us feel welcome along side some of the old cowboys in dirty boots and ancient hats. Many of those same cowboys were longtime friends of both Will and Mr. Marland.

I can't help but feel a special closeness to the Pioneer Woman, a gracious, strong lady that looks out over Oklahoma plains from her place of honor in Ponca City. I feel a connection born on that day so long ago when our famous uncle provided us with many wonderful memories. I can still sense the approval of the adoring crowd that pressed toward the stage. They wanted to be as close as possible to an Oklahoma legend who, true to form, found it fun to surprise thousands with his appearance that early spring day in 1930.

Polo and a New Airport for Claremore

In addition to visiting as many Oklahoma relatives as possible whenever he flew home, Uncle Will would catch up on his other interests in the area, too. Among the many things he was involved with, in and around Rogers County, was the polo team at the Oklahoma Military Academy (OMA) in Claremore. The school was then popularly known as "The West Point of the Southwest." In the fall of 1931, Will himself had joined the OMA polo team for a match, scoring six goals in competition against riders far younger. Three years later, he would arrange for the OMA group, known as The Flying Cadets, and their horses to travel by train to Southern California. Uncle Will's cousin, Dr. Jesse Bushyhead, a Claremore physician, went along as chaperone. The Cadets were to play the Stanford University polo team, which at the time, included Will, Jr., Will's oldest son.

Before a crowd studded with Hollywood celebrities, OMA's Flying Cadets beat Stanford in the match, winning a 14" tall loving cup dubbed, The Will Rogers Trophy. Although the match was obviously intended to be an annual event, the teams would only meet that one year. Uncle Will died before the second match could be planned.

Uncle Will loved polo, I'm sure because of the sport's connection to horses and riding skills he had honed all of his life. He was very proud of the hometown team which existed because OMA had a ROTC cavalry unit at the Claremore campus. It was Will's connection to the academy that helped lead to comments to town leaders concerning the possibility of building an airport in Claremore. "If you had an airport here," he said, "I would be flying in here, instead of Tulsa all the time. Also, I could bring the polo team (from California) here to play the OMA boys."

"Your uncle really wanted Claremore to have something special," Aunt Betty told us later, "because all of the people there were so special to him."

Sure enough, not even two years later, in July of 1931, Uncle Will flew into to help dedicate a new municipal airport in Claremore. By this time, Will was a major box-office star due to films like *So This is London* and *A Connecticut Yankee.* His studio kept him extremely busy and he had just finished one picture and was supposed to start work on a new one the day after the dedication ceremony. The producer of the films told Will, "I'll let you go to Claremore, if you'll let me send you in a private plane, and you turn around and come right back—and I don't mean visit everyone you know at every airport. You have to come right back."

Will agreed, but he didn't *exactly* go right back to Hollywood. The pilot took him into Tulsa the night before the dedication and then he stayed an extra night following the airport events before returning to California. His visit turned out to be a great memory for his family and friends and the entire community.

When Will arrived at the Tulsa airport for the dedication, Dad picked him up as usual and took him to his room at the new downtown Claremore hotel that bore Will's name. The Will Rogers Hotel was opened in February of 1930 and boasted seventy-eight rooms. The new six-story building had cost $321,000 to build and Uncle Will was pleased at the honor of having the hotel named for him. At the time he said, "I am more proud of my name on it than on a marquee—even London has only three-story hotels."

On the way to the hotel Dad has asked Uncle Will for a favor. He asked if the Hollywood pilot, who had brought Uncle Will in, would mind flying some of the kids in the family from Tulsa to Claremore the next day. Dad had already spoken to the pilot, but wanted to make sure it was okay with Uncle Will.

Early the next morning, Dad drove some excited kids to Tulsa. I was one of them. The four oldest children in the extended family made the trip: me, sister Mimi, and our Neal cousins, Jim and Betty. This experience nearly topped the fun we had in the attic with Will's trunk and the ice cream trips made with Uncle Will. What a thrill it was to ride in that beautiful four-passenger plane.

The dedication of the Claremore airport held on July 14, 1931, was a spectacular event. Not only was Uncle Will on hand, but also his friend Wiley Post, who continued to set records. Post had just created a big stir by winning the National Air Race Derby, piloting his plane, the *Winnie Mae* from Los Angeles to Chicago in record time. Then, as mentioned, two weeks before, Post, along with Gatty, had clocked eight days, fifteen hours and fifty-one minutes for their famous flight around the world, setting a new record.

Top flyers like Post and Gatty were internationally known celebrities and at the height of fame when they came to Claremore that summer. Showing up to help dedicate the airport, with Uncle Will as master of ceremonies, they were met by throngs of kids and adults alike. Will famously said that there were "thirty acres of people present," and I do recall how the crowd seemed to stretch clear to the horizon. I also remember how honored I felt to meet Wiley Post and Harold Gatty and shake their hands. We didn't bother them for autographs; that wasn't done much back then, but we felt very privileged to be around the famous men.

After the dedication, Uncle Will returned to the Will Rogers Hotel, and the pilot took the plane back to Tulsa for the evening. On that flight, he had four other members of our family: my younger sisters, Maude and Jane, and our brother, Bob, along with cousin, Harvey Capp Luckett. Dad drove down to the Tulsa airport, picked them up and brought everyone back in plenty of time to have supper at the hotel with Uncle Will.

What a scene that was. In addition to the family, which was large enough on its own, there were several strays joining us for the meal. In those days, everyone wanted to talk to Will, especially around his hometown, and people seized on any opportunity that came along. So, there was a big and noisy gathering that evening, which Uncle Will seemed to enjoy.

After dinner, the Lanes returned to Bartlesville, the Neals and Aunt Polly headed back to Tulsa, and Uncle Will retired to his special room in the southwest corner of the Will Rogers Hotel, located just off the mezzanine. The next day he flew back to Hollywood and resumed work on his current film.

On the drive back home to Bartlesville after that exciting day with Uncle Will, I couldn't have known that one day, many years in the future, I would live in the Will Rogers Hotel for a time, where memories would abound and call to me from every room and hallway.

My Life After Uncle Will

> "This thing of being a hero, about the main thing to it is to know when to die. Prolonged life has ruined more men than it ever made."
>
> —Will Rogers

As stated in Chapter One, Uncle Will's death on August 15, 1935 was a shock to the entire nation, but, his family especially felt a deep and personal loss. For weeks and months following the funeral and memorial services, it was difficult to believe that this vibrant living legend was gone. The last time I recall seeing Uncle Will was in Tulsa, on one of the trips we made with him to the Western Union office to send off his article. As usual, afterward, he treated me and all the cousins to ice cream at a parlor nearby. To this day, I see him grinning from ear to ear as he watched us enjoy our ice cream treats. Of course, he always had one, too.

There were quiet conversations between family members of how important it would be to never blame Wiley Post for the accident that took the lives of both men. The answer to news people or writers trying to stir up controversy was simple. The airplane crash was a tragic accident, nothing more. In fact, the family has maintained that Wiley Post was one of the most capable pilots in history. Perhaps underrated by some due to the accident in Alaska, Wiley

Post's contributions to aviation history is still unparalleled. He deserves a place of honor and respect in American history. Most of all, the Rogers family has appreciated the unique and lasting friendship between these two larger than life individuals: Wiley Post and Will Rogers.

Wiley Post was buried in Edmond, Oklahoma after lying in state at the Oklahoma State Capitol for two hours on the day of his funeral. Twenty thousand people stood outside in nearly 100 degree heat to honor this fallen hero as his body was taken from the State Capitol rotunda to a waiting hearse. He was also honored by services held in his hometown of Maysville, Oklahoma.

Uncle Will was placed in a mausoleum in California at Forest Lawn until it would be returned later to Oklahoma for burial at the Will Rogers Memorial in Claremore. Will and Betty's little son, Fred, who died at age two, was also in the same mausoleum and would be moved later to the Memorial as well.

The Bartlesville Years

I was a typical teenager growing up in the oil town of Bartlesville, Oklahoma at the time of Uncle Will's death in the late 1930's. I started my junior year in high school just weeks after the airplane crash made headlines around the world. Still stunned by the news of Will's passing, I stayed busy with friends and school and church that year. I had five good friends; the same ones since the 7th grade: Kathryn Reasor, Bettie Landis, Marilee Gash, Sara Margaret Gibney, and Betty Utley.

At some point, ten of us girls decided we wanted to create a club of our own. We called ourselves The Top Hat

Club and that small group went everywhere together; games, shopping, the movies. We also had sleepovers and gathered at each others' homes regularly. We thought we were really something. We found some small rhinestone pins in the shape of top-hats at the five and dime store in Bartlesville and bought all they had. We wore those pins until they nearly fell apart. Our mothers supported our efforts to belong to something special and helped plan some events and fancy luncheons for us with real china and silver.

When my senior year arrived I didn't have a clear direction as to what I wanted to do after high school. The year seemed to fly by and in May of 1937, I was crossing the stage to receive my high school diploma. I graduated in spite of my on-going struggle to get passing grades in math. Graduation was a fun time as our group of friends made the rounds of parties and dances.

I didn't have a special boyfriend while in junior high and high school. We always hung out with the boys who were among our group of friends and enjoyed doing things together. Toward the end of high school however, many of our friends were already considering marriage.

The Love of My Life—James (Jim) Meyer

During the summer of 1937 I met a tall young man with a great sense of humor and the kindest heart. James William Meyer, (Jim), had an easy going personality and he quickly became part of our gang. Jim's family had roots in Kansas where he was born in 1915, but he had graduated from high school in Bristow, Oklahoma. After a brief stay in Oregon, the family moved to Bartlesville where they were leasing and operating Myer's Flower Farm on 11th and Shawnee in Bartlesville. On our first real "date" Jim took me to the Fireman's Ball downtown at the Bartlesville Civic Center during that summer after graduation. He treated me special from the very beginning of our relationship.

I admired Jim for working his way through college. He had previously waited tables and worked at a gasoline station to attend the University of Kansas and was preparing to finish his education at the University of Oklahoma. Again, he would need to work on campus to pay for the classes, but he was determined to get a degree in Business Administration and Business Law. We wrote each other often while he was at the University of Oklahoma and he made it home from school whenever he could.

In the meantime, while Jim was away at school, I took courses at a business college located in offices above the popular Mays Brothers Men's Clothing Store located at 3rd and Johnstone in downtown Bartlesville. There were five Mays Brothers stores located around the state. The following year, I was hired as a receptionist for Dr. Boucher, our local dentist, and Dr. Green, who was an optometrist. I was trained as a dental assistant to Dr. Boucher and also kept his books and mailed out statements: a minor miracle considering my poor math skills, but it wasn't difficult and I enjoyed my work very much.

Our Elopement: "The Worst Saturday" of Dad's Life

After seeing each other for nearly two years, Jim and I were deeply in love and often discussed marriage. Many of our friends had already married and we knew we were going to be husband and wife sooner or later, but Jim was adamant about finishing his college education first. One weekend in November, on impulse more than anything else, we decided we would elope; get married and keep it a secret until he graduated in the spring of that year.

Jim had asked a co-conspirator at the floral shop to make me a pretty corsage and soon we were on our way to a little town in Kansas called Sedan to get our marriage license when Jim suddenly said,

"My gosh! Coke, we don't have a ring. You have to have a ring."

We pulled into a tiny jewelry shop in Caney, Kansas and looked at rings.

"Jim, if I get a wedding ring and wear it, people will know I'm married."

So, we settled on a ring with my birthstone; a lovely little ring with a single topaz setting. Even after I received my wedding rings I wore that ring for years. After many moves, I lost the ring, but will never forget how precious it was to me.

We drove into Sedan, Kansas but, found the county offices closed because it was a Saturday. Undeterred, Jim found out where the county clerk lived, went directly to his home and asked the man to come with us to the court house so we could get a license to be married that day. I'm sure the man would have enjoyed spending time at home on his Saturday off, but he kindly agreed and we were soon walking up the steep steps to the court house. Jim and the clerk were walking a bit ahead of me and had already reached the top of the stairs when Jim came running back down to ask,

"Coke, he wants to know your middle name. What is it?"

After all this time, my beloved fiancée did not know my full name. We would laugh about that through the years. I'm actually surprised he knew my real first name since everyone called me, Coke.

"It's Lolita. My full name is Doris Lolita Lane."

With license in hand, we were legally married in the parsonage at the Sedan United Methodist Church on November 18, 1939. We were so proud of ourselves for pulling it off and filled with excitement over our delicious, scandalous secret.

My father was a fan of Oklahoma University football and followed the Sooners faithfully. That year, 1939, the Sooners were on their way to an undefeated season when they played the Tigers of the University of Missouri at their stadium on Saturday, November 18th, the same day Jim and I married. The game was hard fought, but Missouri came out on top with the final score of 7 to 6. Because of the loss, Dad was in a grumpy mood already that weekend.

Jim and I had no idea that all marriage licenses issued around the counties in and around Bartlesville were printed in the Bartlesville newspaper. Sure enough, there for all to see in the next edition of the paper was the announcement that Doris Lolita Lane and James William Meyer were issued a marriage license on November 18th in Sedan, Kansas. The news swept like wildfire through

Bartlesville. Our friends were calling, neighbors were talking, and it didn't take long before Mother and Dad knew. The secret was out.

Dad did not suppress his disappointment. "This is terrible," he said, "here O.U. lost and I lost Coke on the same day! It's the worst Saturday of my life."

Finally, the hubbub settled and after the surprise wore off, Mom and Dad welcomed Jim into the family. He returned from school over Thanksgiving break and my folks hosted a very nice reception for us the day after Thanksgiving. Most of our friends were around for the holiday so we were happy to see them at the reception. All's well that ends well, and our marriage, "took." We were married for sixty-five years until Jim's death in 2004.

The next year, 1940, Jim's parents moved to Sedalia, Missouri to own and operate their own floral shop.

Outbreak of War

Jim worked for Railway Express in Bartlesville during the Christmas holidays that year we were married. Then, after graduating from the University of Oklahoma, he took a job at Phillips Petroleum Company based in Bartlesville. I remember thinking that we were rich because he was making $125.00 a month. Soon, Jim was promoted to the motor fuel department where he was responsible for quality control and testing both aviation and car gasoline products for Phillips. He once came home exhausted and on edge. I could tell something was wrong.

"Well, I was testing German aviation fuel today and we had so little I had to be extra careful. I'm worn out from trying to save as much as possible, yet,have enough to get good results," he reported.

Of course, at that time, Hitler and Germany were in the news continuously and many feared that war was probable, we just didn't know when.

We lived in a small garage apartment and I continued to work for the dentists for another year until we discovered our first baby was on the way. Then, President Roosevelt announced the declaration of war against Japan following the cowardly attack on Pearl Harbor on December 7th, 1941. Three days later, on December 11th, Japan's allies, Germany and Italy, declared war on the United States. World War II was underway.

From the small apartment, we moved out to Tuxedo, a small town about five miles from Bartlesville. Jim rode a bicycle to and from work each day so we could save the money he otherwise would have spent on gasoline. We even raised chickens for a while during this time. Then, we moved back into Bartlesville and rented a house on Wyandotte Street.

The birth of our first son on September 12, 1942 was a joyous event. We were proud parents of William Robert Meyer, whom we called, Billy Bob, and the family adored the little guy. However, the war effort was in full swing and many men were being drafted. Sure enough, Jim received notice that he was going to be drafted, so we quickly made plans to move me and Billy Bob in with my parents for the duration of Jim's service. They had extra room in their home because my sisters were out of the home and my brother, Bob, was already in the service. Our younger sister,

Jane married in 1940 and then, the youngest sister, Maude (Pudge), went to Texas to live with Mimi during the war.

Our little family was just getting settled in with Mom and Dad when word came that Jim's occupation was vital to the war effort and therefore he would *not* be drafted. Since we had already moved, Mom and Dad insisted we stay in their home. We lived there through the remainder of the war years.

In addition to the stress of the war, there was a major flood in 1944 and many homes and businesses in Bartlesville were lost. Jim had a good friend he worked with at Phillips whose home was flooded. While repairs were made to the home, the couple and their two children also moved in with us. It was crowded for a few days, but the couple never forgot the kindness Mom and Dad showed to them by offering their home.

By August of 1945 victory had been proclaimed and the long, hard ordeal that saw the entire world involved in war was finally over. Another reason to give thanks that year was the arrival of our second son, Jerry Gunter, born May 18th of 1945.

The Meyers Move to Caney, Kansas

By war's end, Jim had become dissatisfied with his position at Phillips Petroleum, because he saw little possibility for advancement. We had often talked about operating our own floral business since Jim had experience in that area. We began to look around for an established business to purchase and an opportunity soon arose in the small town of Caney, Kansas, north of Bartlesville about twenty miles, just over the Oklahoma/Kansas state line.

Jim and his Dad traveled to Caney to check out the operation and after their positive report, our family purchased the business from a family by the name of Schaeffer and moved to Caney where we would remain for the next twenty-three years as owners and operators of Meyer's Greenhouse and Florists. The deal also included a large seven room home on the property.

Jim's mother and father were operating a little floral business in Pawhuska, Oklahoma by this time, but decided to sell and move to Caney to help us establish the new business. We all lived in the home next to the floral operation. Soon, it became very successful. We were one of the first businesses to have air conditioning—a huge blessing in the scorching heat of Kansas summers. Jim studied different techniques of flower growing and even developed the method by which we could grow mums early for planting and selling out of season. This brought us a windfall of profit because we could supply other florists throughout the area.

Heartbreak in Caney

While we were growing the business, tragedy struck our family in the winter of 1947. Billy Bob, our oldest son, was a happy, adventuresome lad, five years old at the time. I recall December 19th as a bright, beautiful winter's day. Along with our other workers, I was helping to prepare flowers for an upcoming funeral and we were also working on an order for a big Eastern Star installation event. Jim was out cutting carnations. It was the last day of school for children before the Christmas holiday so Billy Bob, too young for school as yet, saw his friends coming home and wanted to go play with them. He rushed into the greenhouse and told one of the workers,

"Tell Mama I'm going across the street to Jimmy's house."

He was off skipping and running toward the street that ran along side the floral shop. I had seen him do it before. He would jump over the low fence just before the street and then run across to his little friend's home on the other side. Mercifully, that day I was not watching. Billy Bob barely reached the road when an on-coming car came over the hill, hit him, and knocked him several feet along the pavement. Inside the car was a couple from Bartlesville by the name of Jenkins. They were traveling back home after a trip over to Coffeyville, Kansas when Billy Bob darted out onto the highway. They immediately stopped. Mrs. Jenkins had actually been my Sunday School teacher when I was a young girl, years before. Shaken and tearful, the Jenkins took the accident very hard.

"Billy got hit. Billy got hit by a car," one of the kids came shouting.

I ran as fast as my feet could carry me, praying all the way. At the same time, Jim ran to get our car and I held our son as we drove to the nearby hospital in Caney. It was Friday afternoon. We were frantic for help but the doctor, Mike Scimeca, was not in, only a nurse by the name of Verna Harris was on duty. Verna quickly called for Dr. Coon, a semi-retired doctor in town, who arrived very shortly.

His words pierced me like a dagger, "I am so sorry. The little boy is dead. But, the thing of it is; he would have been a vegetable should he have lived. The head injuries were such that there was serious brain damage."

Billy Bob slipped quickly from us into heaven's arms and my heart broke into a million pieces.

To this day, the indescribable aching returns when I think of the little guy that brought us so much joy. I miss him still. I miss seeing him grow. I miss seeing the man he would have become. I miss the fun, the graduations, the wedding, and the grandchildren that might have been. Because we lost Billy Bob on December 19th, only days before Christmas, there isn't a Christmas that comes and goes that I don't wish he was with us to celebrate. My faith and caring support of family alone kept me sane and steady during those heart wrenching days. Of course, we had our other fine son, Jerry, to care for. He was only two years old when his big brother left us.

Three months after the accident, our pain was eased somewhat with the news that we were expecting another child. The new arrival was to come a year later almost to the very day when we lost Billy Bob. On December 14th, 1948, our third son, James Frederick (Jim), was born in Washington County Hospital. God has been so good to me.

The years seemed to fly by as we raised our sons in Caney. They grew up helping us run the business, living out our lives among "salt of the earth" folks who were kind and caring neighbors and friends. We would leave Caney in 1969.

Daddy's Passing

It seemed for a time that every one in our family was in the flower business. My mother and dad moved to Dewey, Oklahoma after his retirement and bought a little flower shop there to operate. They bought flowers and plants directly from us and would sell them at retail prices in their shop. It was working well and they were enjoying their lives together when Dad had a massive heart attack.

We knew Dad had a bad heart and over the years had become weaker and weaker. He was only in his late sixties, but had to be driven nearly everywhere. He could no longer make the deliveries for the shop and even trips to our place to buy supplies for his store were very difficult. He had been admitted to the hospital for chest pains on October 9th of 1964 and was there when a final heart attack claimed his life.

James Gunter Lane, nephew of Oklahoma's favorite son, Will Rogers, was laid to rest, but memories abound of my dad who could pass for our famous uncle. He had the same friendly, outgoing personality, the same mannerisms. As previously noted, he looked so much like Uncle Will that he once fooled a whole crowd who were expecting the famous man in person. We had a special relationship, Dad and I; I missed him, too, so much.

Mother tried to keep the flower shop in Dewey and ran it alone for a while, but it proved to be too much for her. She sold the shop and moved to an apartment in Bartlesville. Mom loved to paint and especially enjoyed china painting. She had kilns in her apartment and had many projects in progress continually.

Both of Jim's parents passed away during our time in Caney. His father had a devastating stroke not long after Billy Bob died. Some say he just couldn't get over God taking a child like Billy Bob, instead of an old man like him. After several years of suffering the effects of the stroke, he died in 1957. Grandma Meyer passed away a year later.

Retirement in Arizona, but There's No Place like Home

Jim and I sold the floral business in Caney in 1969 and decided to spend our retirement years in Scottsdale, Arizona. We enjoyed fifteen years there and even dabbled in real estate for a while which proved to be very profitable for us. We also ran a hardware store in the area. Mom had come to visit us in Arizona when she passed away in March of 1982 at the age of eighty-six.

I will always remember how hard Mother worked along side Dad at Sunset Farm. I can picture her singing that song with Uncle Will at Grandma Lane's piano the night she and Dad met. She was a multi-talented woman and I missed her and the wonderful things she brought to our family.

After Mother's death, the call to return home to Oklahoma was strong and after selling five homes, the hardware store, plus our own home, we made our way back to Bartlesville in 1984. Coming back home to friends and family just felt right. My brother, Bob and his wife, Lou lived in Bartlesville and our sister, Jane and husband Mac and their family lived in Miami, Oklahoma. We were able to purchase our new home in Bartlesville outright—a blessing indeed.

Losing My Jim

God granted Jim and me twenty more years together. Jim fell and broke his hip in 2004. He was mending pretty well in the hospital when he had a serious bout with pneumonia. And, if that wasn't enough, while in a rehabilitation facility, he developed the insidious bacterial infection (MERSA) that attacked his already weakened body. The doctors finally got it under control but, I had already concluded that I would not be able to care for Jim any longer at home. Then, the deadly infection flared up again.

My strong-willed husband kept trying to get out of the hospital bed on his own which led to another fall and another broken hip. Sadly, Jim began to slip away from us. He stopped eating and refused his medicine. It seemed he just became too tired to fight the illnesses that had taken such a toll. On July 16, 2004, my first love, my best friend and life long companion, my intelligent bridge-playing traveling buddy, the caring father and husband we all loved, drew a final breath and was gone. We buried Jim in the little cemetery in Caney, Kansas, where his mom and dad are, and where are beloved little son, Billy Bob, was laid to rest. There is a spot for me, too when my time comes.

Back to the Will Rogers Hotel in Claremore

While Jim was in the nursing home, I had arranged to sell our Bartlesville home without ever letting him know. I ate breakfast with him each morning, but just never could bring myself to tell him I was packing up and preparing to sell our home and move. I called our children and asked them to come and go through the house and take what they wanted. I knew I would be downsizing and wouldn't need much in the small apartment I had found. It turned out to be a wise decision.

I stayed briefly at the Tall Grass Estates, a retirement center in Bartlesville, but the center eventually felt more like a nursing home and I was still very active at the time, so, my good friend from the Pocahontas Club, Ollie Starr, convinced me to move to Claremore where she was living. The old Will Rogers Hotel (yes, the same one that featured Uncle Will's statue in the lobby) had been made into a nice facility called, The Will Rogers Senior Center. It was close to Chelsea and my Pocahontas Club friends.

As I moved into my apartment at the Center in Claremore, it felt like going home again. As mentioned, I was still active and in good health and did a lot of traveling with friends to Tulsa and all around the area. I was eighty-seven years old, but could not only keep up, but was often leading the pack. I would spend the next five years living in the place where I had so many wonderful memories with Uncle Will and the Center was close to the Will Rogers Memorial where I was a docent. The memorial staff refers to the docents as "Ropers" with the unique charge of "keeping the Will Rogers legacy alive." I would be called upon to lead tours or to offer personal insight to those training to be guides or volunteers at the Museum.

Acting my Age

I had a bad fall of my own in the early part of 2011, and of course, I am not getting any younger. So, my youngest son, Jim, and his wife, Sue, who have a home in Bartlesville, invited me to move in with them. Since August of 2011, I have lived with Jim who is now retired; he and Sue have been more than kind to this old gal. I often say, "I put up with them, and it's even more of a miracle that they put up with me."

My oldest son, Jerry, lives with his wife Suzie in Liberty, Kansas. They live in a beautiful old home passed down through the generations from Suzie's family. Jerry stayed connected to the family's love of horticulture by working in forest generation. He represents the fourth generation of Meyers in the floral business. He currently sells greenhouse supplies and seeds to businesses in a large area of the country which includes Oklahoma, Arkansas, Louisiana, Mississippi, and Tennessee. Jerry and Suzie have two children: a daughter, Kinis who is a teacher and counselor in the IT Department at Haskell University in Lawrence, Kansas. Their son, Kirk, earned a business degree at Haskell and now works for the Bureau of Indian Affairs. Kirk lives in Nashville and oversees the construction of bridges and roads throughout Tennessee and all the way from Florida up through Maine.

Jim, with whom I now live in Bartlesville, was stationed at Mc Connell Air Force Base in Wichita, Kansas during the Vietnam War and had the important duty of inspecting flight equipment for our military personnel. As stated, he is now retired. Jim and Sue have three children:

Stacey Lynn, a graduate of The University of Oklahoma with a degree in chemical engineering. Stacey is a regional director for a large cement holding company in Dallas, Texas. Their second daughter, Melissa Joe, is married to Gary Myers and has two children from a previous marriage: Julia, 12, and William, 11 years old. She is a special education teacher and lives with her family in McKinney, Texas. Then, lastly, Jim and Sue's son, Joshua James (Josh), lives at home and like many his age is into computers and music.

If you are keeping count, that makes five grandchildren and two great grandchildren. I am very proud of all my "chickens." I no longer drive, but I have the children and grandchildren I can depend on to haul me around any time I ask. I feel blessed that I am not alone, but still have plenty of family and friends to share these years. I stay active in the Bartlesville Indian Women's Club, my Cherokee district association, as well as my 55Plus Activity Club and my Kum Dubl Methodist Sunday school class.

Wasn't it just yesterday that I saw Uncle Will grab my grandmother's hand and twirl her around the parlor to show us some new dance steps he had seen on Broadway? And it couldn't be so long ago when Mimi and I climbed the stairs at Sunset Farm and fell asleep in our feather bed. Where did the years go?

Fitting Tributes to a Life Well-Lived

"So buy a ranch somewhere in the West. All your life every man has wanted to be a cowboy. Why play Wall Street and die young when you can play cowboy and never die?"

—Will Rogers

A Final Gift from Uncle Will

During the days that followed Uncle Will's death, the family, including my dad and mother, had gathered at Will and Betty's California ranch home. One evening when most everyone else was gone, Aunt Betty, called Dad aside and asked him to follow her upstairs to the bedroom she had shared with Uncle Will. There on a dresser Dad saw a stack of publicity photos of Will taken while he was under contract with 20th Century Fox.

"Those are the last pictures Will ever signed," Betty told my father. "The day he was leaving for Seattle with Wiley, I insisted that he stop packing long enough to autograph eighteen of these photos for his great nieces and nephews. You take them home and give them to the children, or Belle can mail them."

As it turned out, Betty had also asked Will to sign some autograph books belonging to the children of Amon

Carter, the publisher of the *Fort Worth Star-Telegram* at the time, who was Will's good friend. But, after signing the eighteen pictures for us, he said,

"Betty, I don't want to fool with that right now. I'll do it after I get back."

He wouldn't make it back to sign those books for the Carter kids, but those pictures signed for us became beloved heirlooms for me and all of my cousins. I still have mine.

Aunt Betty Returned Often to Oklahoma

Betty Rogers was always family oriented, and she stayed connected to the Oklahoma clan after Will's death by writing and visiting often. She would come to stay with Aunt Sallie or Aunt Estell for days at a time. I still have a picture taken during one of Aunt Betty's visit in 1942. She is holding our son, Billy Bob, not long after he was born.

When a commission was formed and talks were underway for establishing a museum here in Oklahoma to honor Uncle Will, Betty returned for those meetings held several times a year. In a remarkably generous gesture, she offered the land she and Will had purchased near Claremore to be the site of the new Will Rogers Memorial Museum. Will and Betty had planned to build their retirement home on the property but, after his passing, she willed the land to the foundation established to erect the museum. A mausoleum was to be included on the site also. Will had purchased the twenty acres back in 1911 for $5 an acre.

In the beginning, we believe that Aunt Betty thought Will's memorabilia would be housed in a relatively small area. When she realized that the entire museum was to be dedicated to Uncle Will she got busy. She sent clothes that Uncle Will had worn, items of memorabilia from Will's early days, ropes, saddles, awards, miscellaneous letters and notes written in Will's hand, and so much more. Aunt Betty knew these items would be treasured and preserved in a safe and caring environment.

Aunt Betty suggested to the commission that Paula McSpadden Love be named to oversee the building of the memorial. Paula was the daughter of Will's sister, Sallie McSpadden. At the time, Paula and husband Bob, who was a builder and architect, were newlyweds busy building a new home in Vinita, Oklahoma. However, after receiving Aunt Betty's call to head up the project, both of them became dedicated to designing a timeless memorial to honor Uncle Will.

A Unique Memorial to Will in the Colorado Mountains

Before the memorial to Uncle Will was opened in Claremore another memorial was erected and dedicated in 1936 high atop Cheyenne Mountain in Colorado Springs, Colorado. The site, called the Will Rogers Shrine of the Sun, consists of a small plaza displaying the bronze bust of Will Rogers and an 80-foot tower with a perpetual flame. The place on the mountain was donated by a wealthy philanthropist by the name of Spencer Penrose who was a friend of Will's. Originally, the site was to be used as a gravesite for Mr. Penrose, however, after Will's death, Penrose wanted the spot to be a tribute to Will.

Just two years later when Penrose died, his ashes were entombed at the shrine as well.

The bronze bust was sculpted by Jo Davidson, another friend of Uncle Will's. Davidson had tried to get Will to "sit" for a sculpting session but Uncle Will had always put him off, saying,

"Don't worry, Jo. We'll get it done some day."

With Will's passing, the sculptor worked closely with Aunt Betty to make sure the details were accurate. She even lent the artist some of Will's clothes to use for reference.

The dedication of the memorial in Colorado was a grand affair. Several members of the family were present including Mother and Dad. Aunt Sallie, Aunt Lasca, and W. M. "Clu" Gulager, our cousin from Muskogee attended. Clu had been close to Will. His mother, Aunt Martha, was the sister of Mary Schrimsher, Will's mother. Later, Clu's brother John, and wife, Hazel, had a son they also named Clu; some may recall he went on to become a well-known television and movie actor.

The ceremony began with a "buckskin horse, his saddle empty," stepping into the plaza of the shrine. The following story appeared in the Colorado Springs Gazette on September 7, 1937. A few of the details were wrong as noted below:

> The chimes of the shrine tower played low, solemn notes while those in the crowd assembled to dedicate the shrine to the memory of the beloved cowboy philosopher bowed their heads.

> Tears came to the eyes of Mrs. T.W. (actually should be J.T.) McSpadden of Chelsea, Oklahoma, Will Rogers' only surviving sister... Tears showed, too, in the eyes of Mrs. Lasca Lane Luckett of Colorado Springs, daughter of Will Rogers' brother (Lasca was the daughter of Will Roger's sister).
>
> Standing by Mrs. McSpadden's chair, because there were not enough seats for relative guests, Gunter Lane, Rogers' nephew, glumly chewed gum.
>
> Lane, from Claremore, Oklahoma (we were actually in Bartlesville at this time), the rope-twirling sage's home town, had facial features and manners strongly reminiscent of Will Rogers himself...

That last line always makes me think of the time Dad was pressed into service as a Will Rogers-style speaker at the American Legion convention.

A big three-day Will Rogers Memorial Rodeo and parade were held in conjunction with the opening of the shrine, so my parents got to see and visit with a lot of the old cowboys they knew; many of them, of course, had known Uncle Will so well. As the newspaper story suggests, Aunt Lasca and Uncle Hap were already living in Colorado. Aunt Laska (Winky) ended up being employed by the shrine's creator, Mr. Penrose. For two years she acted as hostess and greeter for people visiting the Will Rogers Shrine of the Sun.

On the day of the dedication, Aunt Lasca was the person who officially revealed the beautiful bronze bust of

Uncle Will. The *Colorado Springs Gazette* story described the moment:

> Lasca Lane pulled aside the shroud by its ribbons, and the dry-witted Will looked southeast towards Oklahoma, his home country.

All Dressed Up For the Opening of the Will Rogers Memorial Museum

While the Memorial Museum in Claremore was in the works, the Oklahoma legislature appropriated $200,000 to go toward its construction. Sometimes overlooked, however, is the outpouring of help from the public, who wanted to see a memorial erected to honor their beloved Will. Although America was in the throes of the Great Depression, according to a *Tulsa World* newspaper story by Edward J. Burks from November 5, 1938:

"Five hundred seventy-five thousand men, women and children made voluntary contributions ... which the Will Rogers Memorial commission will use in creating a lasting memorial to Will Rogers, a memorial intended to perpetuate something of his philosophy of life. Contributions to the fund averaged about 45 cents each and amounted to a total of $266, 121."

I will never forget the opening of the Will Rogers Memorial Museum on November 4th of 1938, a day chosen because it was Uncle Will's birthday. We were all dressed up and ready to drive down from Bartlesville to Claremore with Dad at the wheel, when a neighbor girl,

Harriet Harlow, came by. She and her family were our close friends.

"C'mon, Harriet," my father said. "Jump in the car and go with us to Claremore." That was Dad, always ready to load people in and take them along … the more, the merrier.

Harriet ran to ask her mother, who said, "Change dresses, and you can go."

It was a beautiful autumn day, and as we drove along, I noticed the leaves already changing to shades of orange and red and yellow. We arrived early and went around to the little park just south of the Memorial building where hay bales had been scattered around to provide places for people to sit. Everyone attending that day, and there were thousands, were treated to barbecue sandwiches, soda pop, and water, all for free. The family's rancher friends had furnished the beef and the smell of it cooking in the pits around the Memorial area wafted up to us as we walked along the grounds.

My cousin, Mary, Will's only daughter, came with the rest of Will's immediate family to the dedication. She was six years older than me, but Mimi and I enjoyed getting a chance to hang around with her during all the festivities.

The Memorial staff had set aside a special section on the terrace for all of Will's family. We all sat looking up at a big table which held dozens of microphones. It was reminiscent of the dedication of the airport in Claremore six years earlier. Nationwide radio hookups allowed people ranging from President Roosevelt to show-business figures like Eddie Cantor, George M. Cohan, and Fred

Stone to eulogize Will. The Oklahoma broadcaster, Glenn Condon, sat at the table in the Memorial, coordinating broadcasts from across the country. Also present were representatives of the Indian tribes of Oklahoma and a Cherokee Choir performed during the program. At the table also were Will's sons, Will Jr. and Jimmy. Just behind them sat Aunt Betty, Sallie McSpadden, and Mary.

Paula McSpadden Love had done a wonderful job organizing the event and I remember how she herded us around, keeping the family together, going up and down the stairs of the Memorial with us even though she had been afflicted with polio as a child. That didn't slow her down a bit. Paula would later gather materials for a lovely book of Uncle Will's quotes titled, *The Will Rogers Book*. She would be the curator of the Will Rogers Memorial from 1938 when it was dedicated, until her death in the early 1970's. No one in the family had been closer to Will and Betty. She served the memory of Uncle Will with love and respect. Paula and her husband left the Museum in good shape for the director who followed: Dr. Reba Collins.

Dr. Collins was also a wonderful guardian of Will's legacy who served the Museum from 1975 to 1989. Following Dr. Collins tenure, the Museum underwent major refurbishments in the 1990's while Joseph Carter served as Director from 1989 to 1999. Then Michelle Lefebvre-Carter became Director of the Museum from 2000 until November of 2006. Currently, Mr. Steven Gragert, is another wonderful director of the Will Rogers Memorial, a beautiful facility visited by thousands each year. Every

Oklahoman should visit once; they would be so proud of the impact Will made on the nation and even the world.

Another statue of Will Rogers is erected on the campus of Texas Tech University in Lubbock, Texas. Amon Carter, Will's longtime friend mentioned earlier, hailed from west Texas and campaigned for the placement of the statue with the following inscription on the base, *"Lovable Old Will Rogers on his favorite horse, 'Soapsuds', riding into the Western Sunset."* Dedicated in 1950, the statue of Will astride his favorite horse, stands 9 feet and 11 inches high and weighs around 3,200 pounds. The students wrap Will and Soapsuds in red crepe paper for every home football game and occasionally wrap the famous pair in black when national tragedies occur.

Then, still yet, another statue of Uncle Will owns a prominent place in the National Statuary Collection at the United States Capitol Building. Created by the same Jo Davidson who sculpted the bronze bust for the Shrine of the Sun, it is also viewed by thousands of visitors to Washington, D. C. each year. On June 6th, 1939 the statue was dedicated with more than 2,000 people in attendance including Aunt Betty, their children and other family members. For generations to come, the statue will have particular significance to Congress and every President of the United States.

Besides the memorials to Uncle Will in stone, many paintings by famous artists have captured his likeness; among them Charles Russell and Charles Banks Wilson. Wilson's life-size painting of Will, standing on a grassy airstrip under a beautiful blue sky, hangs in the Oklahoma State Capitol Building.

Betty came back so often to the museum that they built a little apartment on to the gate house to accommodate her when she visited. The children, Will Jr. and Jimmy came back often, too. Jimmy and his first wife even chose to come out on their honeymoon. All of the children were interested in the Memorial and their father's legacy.

Mary, Will and Betty's only daughter, who had a particularly hard time with Uncle Will's passing, lived a colorful life. She married three times, the last time to wealthy business man, Walter Brooks. The couple divorced after only two years of marriage and Mary traveled extensively and lived in Europe many years. She became ill in 1989 while she was living overseas. She called her brother, Jim when she discovered she was ill, letting him know that she wanted to return home. "I don't want to die over here, Jim, I want to come home." So, Jim went over and helped Mary move back home to California just before she died in 1989 from cancer at a hospital in Santa Monica.

Will is Finally Lovingly Laid to Rest in Oklahoma

A group of five Oklahoma business men donated the money to design and build the sunken garden area that would be home to the Will Rogers Family Mausoleum on the Will Rogers Memorial grounds. Will's body was placed there in 1944, then Aunt Betty, who passed away in 1944, is there, too. Will and Betty's children, Mary, Jimmy and his first wife, Astria, along with Fred, the young son lost to diphtheria at the age of two, are entombed at the site. Will Rogers, Jr. is buried along side his wife in Tubac, Arizona. His wife's parents had been missionaries to the Indians in Arizona. The couple lived in Tubac for many years and according to his wife's wishes, were laid to rest with her family who had served the Native Americans there.

I return to the Memorial as often as possible, it is a great blessing to me. I've walked its corridors many times, sometimes informally, other times by invitation or as part of a celebration. For instance, I go once a year with the members of the Pocahontas Club to place a basket of fall foliage beside Will's statue in the rotunda, and a wreath on his tomb, in the ground's gardens. You'll recall that Uncle Will was one of the few men ever granted membership in the club; at this writing, the members of my family who are also members of the Pocahontas Club include a dozen great-great nieces and one granddaughter, Bette Rogers Brandon, who currently lives in California. In this special way I remain connected to my past, my future, and all of my dear family members.

I think often of the special love shared between Betty and Uncle Will. It is indeed a shame that they didn't have many more years together, but certainly, they are together forever at the Will Rogers Memorial. It is my sincere hope that for generations to come, folks will visit the Memorial to experience, understand, and enjoy the legend who was Will Rogers; an Oklahoma cowboy who became one of the most famous and beloved men in the world.

Going Home Again: Back To Sunset Farm

> "On my way home to Oklahoma. What's happier, especially if people have forgotten what you used to be."
>
> —Will Rogers

The old home is still there; I've seen it many times. The house at Sunset Farm is a portal to my past; a past I believe worth remembering and repeating to those who will come after me. The beautiful old three story home is the framework for all the information included in these pages. At the same time Uncle Will was becoming one of the most famous and beloved entertainers known around the world, I was privileged to be a part of his wonderful unique family.

As far back as the 1950's, whenever a friend or family member wanted, we would take a drive out to the house that still sits in Chelsea, Oklahoma on land that was once Sunset Farm. From the road in front of the house I would tell fellow travelers some of the things I remembered, as we looked on from the outside. My memories of those days and that place always spill out and run together. It is sometimes difficult to describe my feelings and love for the old place which, to me, sits on sacred ground.

A group of us would sometimes get out of the car and walk around the house to the backyard and I would point out the different rooms, including the back porch where we slept in the summer. As we walked, I would share the stories of Granny's last Christmas; the big cedar tree with the beautiful electric lights Uncle Will and Aunt Betty sent us; about the time we moved Granny's hospital bed to the upstairs room that Mimi and I shared, so she could see the Christmas lights. I loved telling others about sunlit summer days when we would play outdoors until dark forced us inside. The hundreds of childhood adventures that took us from one end of the farm to the other still make me smile and even laugh out loud at times. Each visit conjured up visions of how we would squeal with delight as we swung out on the rope in the barn; how we hopped aboard to ride along with Monday on the milk wagon; the many hours of pretend play using items from Uncle Will's vaudeville trunk; I even have fond memories while working hard during canning season.

For eighty years, ever since we left the farm in 1929, I yearned to see the house inside, but never had the nerve to walk up to the door uninvited and ask to come in. It wasn't until 2009 that I finally had the opportunity. One special friend, Ollie Starr, urged me to contact the current owners to ask if I could possibly get a peak inside the home.

Finally, a Look Inside

Ollie and I were eating lunch at the Chelsea Senior Center in early August of 2009 when she suggested we stop in at the newspaper office afterward.

Ollie and I are both active members of the Pocahontas Club, the special group of Cherokee women I have mentioned previously. She knew of my deep desire to see the home and was interested in helping make that happen from the beginning. We met briefly with Linda Lord, the editor of the *Chelsea Reporter*, and told her of my desire to see inside my childhood home. Linda told us the current owner of the home was a man by the name of Ken Grey. "Ken has a machine shop here in Chelsea and I can tell you where it is," she offered.

That was all Ollie needed. "Let's go by and see the man, Coke."

We arrived at Mr. Grey's shop, but he was not in that day. Instead, his son, a young man who had recently returned from serving a tour in Iraq, graciously offered to help.

"Just get in touch with my mother. I'm sure a visit can be arranged. Here is their home number and Mom's cell phone number."

A few days later I called Mrs. Grey with my request. Mrs. Alfreda Grey agreed to meet me at the house for a look inside. I asked to bring a few close friends along, and, like her son, Mrs. Grey was very kind and understanding.

So, on the afternoon of August 4, 2009, my friend, Carolyn Wilcott agreed to drive Ollie and I and another dear friend, Linda Bradshaw out to tour the home that meant so much to me. Another good friend, Farrell Prater, joined us, too. Linda actually was a docent at the Will Rogers Memorial in Claremore and knew more about Uncle Will's life and family than just about anyone. I had mentioned to Linda several times that I wished I could visit the house and she always said,

"If you ever get to do it, I'd really like to come along."

While the five of us traveled to the home which I would forever know as Granny Lane's place, I thought how the day was even more significant because it was my little sister's birthday. On that day in 1926, Maud Estelle (nicknamed, "Pudge") was born in the home. My feet had skipped across the floor of that house with the grace of a young girl when I had last stepped inside. Now I was heading into my nineties.

A few minutes before 3 o'clock in the afternoon we arrived at the home, parked the car in the backyard under a big shade tree and walked across the grass and up the four steps to the back porch. Even while taking the steps gingerly now because of my age, I remembered how, as a little girl, I once bounded onto the back porch, taking the steps two at a time. The little girl inside me would be along for every moment of this sweet step back in time. I asked God to give me the strength to walk through each room and climb the stairs once again.

Alfreda Grey was there to meet us, along with a well-behaved small boy she was babysitting for her daughter and another very nice lady who was Alfreda's neighbor. They welcomed us and I took a long, deep breath as I crossed the threshold into another world. I stood for a moment, poised between the present world and that world of my youth. I was home again.

My first impressions were about the things that were *not* on the back porch. *Eighty years ago there had been a cream separator right there. Where are all the shelves and the milk bot-*

tles? My friends were watching and waiting for my reaction, but, all I could think of were little things that were missing: the old utensils we used, pegs for our aprons, the towels that hung nearby. The porch had been converted into a sitting room, but in my mind's eye, I saw Mimi and me, washing our hands with lye soap. I saw the dish pan full of boiling water and the stools we would sit on to clean the separator.

We moved from there into the kitchen.

"Mrs. Grey," I said. "The kitchen has been done over beautifully."

Amazingly the woodwork I remembered from the 1920's had been retained, although the butler pantry had been removed at some point to make the space larger. The voices came back to me with force. I could hear the happy chatter around Granny's big, sturdy kitchen table as we did our homework or ate family meals. I remembered Granny preparing the many mouth-watering meals for us in between her milking and household chores.

Entering the dining room, I saw Mrs. Grey's large table and commented,

"Oh, wow. You've got a big nice table, too. It's a lot like Granny's."

I recalled the extra 10-inch leaves that were added to Granny's table at holiday time to accommodate fourteen or sixteen people. Granny's table was passed to my mother, who kept it until she moved to an apartment in Bartlesville. It then went to my baby sister, Maud (Pudge), who had it shipped to her home in Seminole, Florida. After she and her husband passed away, their eldest daughter, Marcia Belle Stone, inherited the table. Since the Tucker family gathers at Marcia's home for holidays, the old table is still a focal point of joyous get-togethers, a century after Granny and Granddad Lane first acquired it. Again, I was glad to see that some of the fancy woodwork above all the doors had survived. But, to my delight, the bay window was still in intact. Many hours were spent sitting at that window while we read of far away places, dreamed our dreams, and thought of all we wanted to be and do.

I had heard that a good part of the home had been ravaged by a fire in 1995. Now, moving into the living room, I saw that this room had been one nearly destroyed by the blaze. *Wasn't it just yesterday that the fire from the fireplace cast a warm glow to the living room and the beautiful gold gilded mirror sparkled above the mantel?* This mirror I had kept in my home for many years.

I felt a hand on my arm and I stopped when Farrell said,

"Coke, I think we'd all like to know just what you're feeling right now."

How could I tell them? How could I tell anyone who hadn't been a child in this place what it was like to be back here after eighty years? I wasn't even sure I could explain how I felt to myself. So, after a moment to gather my thoughts, I finally said what was on my mind.

"I'm so excited," I said with a smile. "But, my heart is filled with many emotions and memories of my life in this house. Every time I look around, another one comes rushing in. I'm kind of afraid to talk too much about them."

"Oh, no," Farrell said, the others nodding in agreement. "All of us want to know what your life was like here in this lovely big home."

I smiled again, and, as we moved through the rest of the house, I tried to more openly express my thoughts as I described the memories the house evoked.

As was the case with Granny Lane, Alfreda Grey had a piano and settee in the downstairs parlor, and the sight of those two things brought back another flood of personal memories. At times I spoke of things I recalled, but at other times, I just kept the precious memories to myself. *Right about here*, I thought, *near the front door, was the entry piece. I saw in my mind the tall mirror with a small protruding marble shelf. On the shelf was placed the silver tray which held the calling cards for Granny Lane's many visitors.*

Upstairs I pointed out the room that was Uncle Will's when he came to visit. I tried to describe Granddad's office space and how the sewing lady took that space once a year when she came to sew for the family. I mentioned Aunt Polly's room and the tower room, but I caught my breath when we entered Granny Lane's bedroom. Somehow, all these decades later, the light still danced along the walls in the same way it had when I was a child. *Surely, those couldn't be the same windows.* When I asked, Mrs. Grey smiled and said, "No, but my father-in-law reproduced them. It was a real undertaking. He had to work with more than 300 individual pieces of glass to recreate the windows."

"Well, he did a wonderful job," I said as I remembered carrying the silver tray into Granny who was bed-ridden, so she could go through the calling cards left by friends and neighbors after she became so very ill. The golden light from those windows once again made me feel warm and peaceful as we exited the room.

I knew that the house fire in 1995 had destroyed the attic, but memories of the fun we had up there leapt to my mind and I even looked up toward the ceiling, as if to summon all those happy child-like voices pretending to be stars on the vaudeville stage, just like Uncle Will.

Now the visit was coming to an end, and the strangest, sweetest nostalgia settled over me. We thanked Mrs. Grey for her kindness in allowing us to tour the home. I paused on the front porch to take one more look at the yard that had been my playground more than eighty years before. Happy and sad at the same time, I felt warm tears roll down my face as I gazed at the old iron fence I remembered, along with the gnarled cedar tree by the house. The tree was bent and worn, ravaged by the years, but still proudly standing. I couldn't help but feel I had a lot in common with the weathered old cedar that had experienced so much, yet was still standing after many decades.

Driving away, I took a look over my shoulder once more and the words of Thomas Wolfe's novel came to mind: *You Can't Go Home Again*. Written in 1940 the novel quickly became a part of our culture, reminding us that things and people change and its impossible to return to the way it was in our past. However, with apologies to Mr. Wolfe, I have gone home in my mind time and time again. The visit in person in 2009 made me realize the house had changed in many respects, but my love and appreciation for the old home will never diminish. The vivid and beloved images of Sunset Farm will be with me for as long as I live.

Driving back into Claremore on the famous "Mother Road," old Route 66, I was full of thoughts and feelings triggered by the visit to Sunset Farm, but mainly I was grateful for the nostalgic trip back in time. I entered the lobby of the Senior Center, which once was the Will Rogers Hotel. I smiled up at the statue of my famous great-uncle and, as I had done so many times before, I once again rubbed his shoes for luck. It had been a good, good day.

What if Uncle Will Had Lived to be 100?

Many ask me what the future would have held for Uncle Will if he had lived to old age. Most likely he would have appeared in more movies and continued his syndicated column. His voice would have been heard loud and clear through out World War II and he would have been a proponent of war bonds, rubber drives, and building up our country's military strength. He would have flown over, perhaps with Wiley, to see and entertain the troops overseas. He would have been vocal and proud of America's war effort and would have written about the men and women who became so instrumental in our country's victory.

As he aged, he might have decided to produce movies instead of star in them. Or, he may have become bored with the whole Hollywood scene and given up show business all together. He would have continued to decline the invitations to run for political office, feeling he would have more impact if he wasn't identified with a particular party.

I know for sure that if Uncle Will had lived to retire, he and Aunt Betty would have returned home to Oklahoma. They would have built a fine home on the property in Claremore and yes, I can see him growing old surrounded by family and the same old friends he had known since childhood. But two things, I think he would have insisted upon. One, he would be always open to travel and new adventures. Secondly, his ability and love for writing may have continued into his older years because his commentary was always up to date, relevant, and was the voice of common sense for so many.

Uncle Will would have embraced his golden years, holding on to them and squeezing every last ounce of memorable moments from them. He would have been one of our country's most honored and respected elder statesmen, without ever holding a political office.

What Will Said About Getting Old

As I have grown older I try to remember some of Will's quips about aging. Here are some of my favorites:

> Eventually you will reach a point when you stop lying about your age and start bragging about it.
>
> The older we get, the fewer things seem worth waiting in line for.
>
> Some people try to turn back their odometers. Not me, I want people to know "why" I look this way. I've traveled a long way and some of the roads weren't paved.
>
> When you are dissatisfied and would like to go back to youth, think of Algebra (this is especially true for me—Amen!)

You know you are getting old when everything either dries up or leaks.

I don't know how I got over the hill without getting to the top.

One of the many things no one tells you about aging is that it is such a nice change from being young.

One must wait until evening to see how splendid the day has been.

Being young is beautiful, but being old is comfortable.

If you don't learn to laugh at trouble, you won't have anything to laugh at when you are old.

What I Want My Children and Grandchildren (and Everyone) to Know About the Man I Called 'Uncle Will'

As surely as Sunset Farm and the old home have stayed alive in my memory so have my many memories of Will Rogers. I would hope that state leaders and those who have control of such things, will always strive to preserve and promote his contributions to our nation and in particular, to our great state of Oklahoma. He *is* Oklahoma in so many definable ways.

Will Rogers embodied America at its finest. He was a common man who was yet, so uncommon. Whether he was rope twirling in the rodeo or on the vaudeville stage or meetings kings and queens of nations, he wore the stamp of the common well—it was etched on his character. The old calico shirts, the cowboy hat, the embarrassed grin, the blue eyes that twinkled with a joke; all were makings of an unforgettable figure of stage and screen.

Uncle Will could have settled for what he had so many times. His family was well established and he could have been that boy who grew up on a ranch in Oklahoma. He could have stayed in Oologah, ran Dog Iron Ranch and never left Oklahoma. You see, he was modest yet confident in his ability to have an impact, to change the world, to make a difference. He had a calling; a sense of being different and apart. He had a sense of destiny.

I believe Uncle Will was somewhat of a genius; a special genius, not of strategy, or politics, but of humor and discernment. He was remarkably gifted at sensing what others needed to hear and believe in. How he kept from offending any party or group or man is phenomenal. But, that was Uncle Will. He was a genius at being a real person.

The large and small details of Will Rogers' life make him a genius; I just can't bring myself to call him less. He was my hero as an impressionable little girl. The outpouring of love and grief at his passing confirm that he was a hero to many. Yet, Uncle Will looked so unheroic in some of the old photos and movies. There have been many great paintings of Will, and some capture an aspect of his character, but not all. To tell you the truth, he even looks a little uneasy in those bronze statues. Though wonderful, the statues just can't possibly portray all he was; perhaps the man was just too real, too flesh and blood, and, too much like all of us.

I hope those who read this book come away with a sense that there was once a special Oklahoma family who raised a special son, who had a special impact on the life and times in which he lived. He spoke and wrote simple words that made sense while bringing a smile to the faces of those who heard or read them. The world is better because Will Rogers was in it.

When I pass a mirror, I realize that I resemble Uncle Will; others often comment on the resemblance. I have a prominent nose just like my father and brother, who also looked a lot like Uncle Will. I also own certain mannerisms I'm sure I inherited from the Rogers side of the family. Like Will, I love to read and tell stories and I am always ready for an adventure. I hope I have inherited a bit of Will's great heart, as well. I care deeply about the future of our country and pray she always remains the beacon of freedom and fairness and goodness in the world. As Uncle Will was prone to do, I often cheer for the underdog and want the little guys to win now and then. And, oh yes, like Uncle Will, I love a good joke. I try to find humor in everyday life and believe that laughter has done my heart good "like a medicine," the Bible says.

"One Must Wait Until Evening to See How Splendid the Day has Been" —Uncle Will

Sometimes late at night or very early in the morning when the house is quiet and still, I hear them–the voices of the people I have loved who are now gone: Granny Lane calling us in from play to supper around the big table in the kitchen at Sunset Farm; Uncle Will rarin' back and singing us a song at Granny's piano; Mother and Dad whispering over morning coffee; Mimi begging me, "Please, Coke, come sit with me in the parlor while I practice;" Billy Bob, my precious little boy, taken much too soon, laughing and romping in the bright Kansas sun; Jim, my husband who never once gave me reason to doubt his love; my little sister, Jane who had the sweetest smile; the happy chatter of aunts and uncles and cousins and dear friends who have now passed on. Seems a bit strange that I am still around, but, the good Lord must not be quite through with me yet.

I am ninety two years old at the time of this writing and it's no secret that I am approaching the final years of my life. My steps are a little slower and my hearing isn't quite what it once was, yet, I'm blessed to feel strong, healthy, and happy.

I don't know how many more days I will see the morning sun rise. It is inevitable. There will be a final day, when the sun will set on my life. Uncle Will said, "One must wait until evening to see how splendid the day has been." Well, I don't intend to sit around and wait for it, but the evening will come and when it does … I will look back and see just how splendid all my days have been.

Special Thanks ...

I want to thank my friend, Carolyn Wilcott for helping me with this book. She has done more to get the book to the stage to be published than even me. She taped interviews and transcribed notes on her computer and made corrections time and time again. She personally made the time to listen to my many experiences and memories; encouraging me to "tell it all." I'm very grateful to author, John Wooley, who was instrumental in getting the project under way.

Also, friends Farrell Prather, Ollie Starr and Linda Bradshaw kept me focused on telling these stories so I could leave them for my children and family before they would be lost forever. Thank you dear friends—and I hope you enjoy the book as much as we did making it to the finish. Many family stories and people are left out, I'm sorry to say, but what remains is true as I remember it.

Sincere thanks also to Tate Publishing and especially, Creative Project Director, Rita Tate. They have become dear friends and saw the value of sharing my memories of Uncle Will for generations to come.

—Doris "Coke" Lane Meyer

Summer 2012

1. Doris Lolita Lane, 1920

2. Maud Rogers Lane, Will's sister, Coke's grandmother

3. Capp C. Lane—My Granddad

4. Coke's family 1930's aunt and uncles and cousins

5. Granny Lane's house at Sunset Farm

Phone similar to Granny Lane's "party line" at Sunset Farm

7. Cousins Betty Maud Neal and "Coke" Lane

8. Will Rogers with fellow performer and friend, Tom Mix

"ELECTRIC LIGHTS IN MY OLD HOME TOWN"
by SANDI DYER
CLAREMORE, OKLAHOMA

9. Hotel Will Rogers

10. Will Rogers our "Uncle Will."

11. Coke and husband, Jim Meyer, 1940

Belle and James Gunter Lane
(Mother and Dad) 1945

Coke with sons, William Robert "Billy Bob," (4 years) and Jerry Gunter (2 years); 1946

13. 1946–1969

14. Coke and Jim on 60th anniversary. November 1999

15. Robert "Bob" McSpadden, Coke Lane Meyer, Pat Reeder, "Clem" McSpadden

16. "Cousins by the dozens!" Will Rogers Nov 4th Birthday in Claremore 2004. 128 attended.

17. Coke Meyer in Cherokee dress, 90th birthday; Kennedy Center, Washington, D.C.